As one of the world's longest established and best-known travel brands, Thomas Cook are the experts in travel.

For more than 135 years our guidebooks have unlocked the secrets of destinations around the world, sharing with travellers a wealth of experience and a passion for travel.

Rely on Thomas Cook as your travelling companion on your next trip and benefit from our unique heritage.

Thomas Cook **pocket** guides

DUBROVNIK

Written by Helena Zukowski, updated by Jeroen van Marle
Original photography by Helena Zukowski

Published by Thomas Cook Publishing
A division of Thomas Cook Tour Operations Limited
Company registration no. 3772199 England
The Thomas Cook Business Park, Unit 9, Coningsby Road,
Peterborough PE3 8SB, United Kingdom
Email: books@thomascook.com, Tel: +44 (0) 1733 416477
www.thomascookpublishing.com

Produced by Cambridge Publishing Management Limited
Burr Elm Court, Main Street, Caldecote CB23 7NU
www.cambridgepm.co.uk

ISBN: 978-1-84848-436-8

© 2006, 2008 Thomas Cook Publishing
This third edition © 2011
Text © Thomas Cook Publishing
Maps © Thomas Cook Publishing/PCGraphics (UK) Limited

Series Editor: Karen Beaulah
Production/DTP: Steven Collins

Printed and bound in Spain by GraphyCems

Cover photography © Dennis Cox/Alamy

Although every care has been taken in compiling this publication, and the contents
are believed to be correct at the time of printing, Thomas Cook Tour Operations
Limited cannot accept any responsibility for errors or omissions, however caused,
or for changes in details given in the guidebook, or for the consequences of any
reliance on the information provided. Descriptions and assessments are based on
the author's views and experiences when writing and do not necessarily represent
those of Thomas Cook Tour Operations Limited.

CONTENTS

SYMBOLS KEY

The following symbols are used throughout this book:

ⓐ address ☎ telephone ⓦ website address ⓔ email
🕐 opening times Ⓝ public transport connections ❶ important

The following symbols are used on the maps:

🛈 information office		point of interest	
🛫 airport		○ city	
🚍 bus station		○ large town	
🚆 railway station		○ small town	
✝ cathedral		═ motorway	
❶ numbers denote featured		━ main road	
cafés & restaurants		━ minor road	
		─ railway	

Hotels and restaurants are graded by approximate price as follows:
£ budget price ££ mid-range price £££ expensive

▶ *Walk on the ancient walls of the city*

INTRODUCING
Dubrovnik

Introduction

So many words of praise have been heaped on Dubrovnik, which is known as the 'pearl of the Adriatic', that it has always shone like a beacon in the world of tourism. As part of the former Yugoslavia, it was an enormously popular sun-and-sea destination; no one was prepared for the economic problems that resulted from plummeting tourism during the Balkan wars. Over the past decade, however, the word that Croatia is back in business has been spreading like honey on a hot summer's day. Thanks to the welcoming nature of the Croatians, and a programme of studiously authentic rebuilding, the charm of Dubrovnik has reasserted itself and visitors can experience this captivating culture once again.

Part of the city's eternal allure may be the questions and contradictions that cling to it. How, for example, did Dubrovnik manage to hang on to its majestic city walls in the 19th century when every other city in Europe was tearing theirs down? How do the waters that lap Croatia's rugged coastline remain so incredibly clear and full of fish? How can a country that celebrates religious festivals with such fervour also be Europe's top naturist destination? And how has Dubrovnik managed to remain intact after so many centuries of invasion?

Like Prague, Dubrovnik always kept an eye on the future: when invaders flocked in and threatened to wreak havoc in the city, the citizens paid the conquerors to leave them alone. These invaders, who came from cities such as Venice, Istanbul, Budapest and Vienna, sometimes stayed and put down roots, leaving their imprint on the culture. It's no wonder that the citizens developed a great yearning to be part of the Western world. Now, as part of independent Croatia, the citizens of Dubrovnik feel sure that they will blend in seamlessly when the country joins the European Union in the near future.

Before the 1991 war, Croatia had long been home to minority populations, but in the 2001 census more than 90 per cent of the population identified itself as ethnically Croat. Croats warmly welcome visitors, and are committed to putting the horrors of the war and ethnic tensions behind them. The painstakingly restored Dubrovnik is, once again, in the words of George Bernard Shaw, a 'paradise on earth'.

◔ *The red-tiled roofs and imposing walls of Dubrovnik*

When to go

The ideal times to visit Dubrovnik are usually May or the late summer and early autumn months. By then the major tourist push is over, yet the sea will still be warm and the days pleasantly balmy. Average temperatures in May are 23°C (73°F); in September the average is 27°C (81°F) and in October 22°C (72°F). For those interested in lots of activities and enjoying a range of nightlife options, August is the best month to go, although it can be very hot and crowded then. Dubrovnik in winter has an almost poetic charm: just walking around the city at that time of the year can be an enchanting experience, and it's not too cold – the average January temperature is usually around 9°C (48°F).

SEASONS & CLIMATE

On the Adriatic coast, Dubrovnik enjoys a Mediterranean climate, with hot, dry summers and mild spring and autumn weather. Winter is generally a bit cooler, with occasional rain.

The tourist season generally runs from April to October, with spring and summer the best time to enjoy activity holidays, including biking or hiking. The sea is usually warm enough for swimming between mid-May and early October.

ANNUAL EVENTS
January & February
Dubrovnik Carnival Fest For the best part of two months, the city gets festive, and the carnival in Dubrovnik is how many people think life in general should be – mainly concerned with dressing up. Details of particular events and locations are available from the tourist information office (see page 152). Ⓦ www.karnevalfest.hr

February
Feast of St Blaise (3 Feb) The city's patron saint (see page 10)
is celebrated with a procession around town.

March & April
Libertas Film Festival Since 2005, Dubrovnik's week-long film festival
has presented new Croatian and international films, attracting
thousands of locals and foreigners, including many celebrities.
Screenings are at three indoor and outdoor locations around town.
Ⓦ www.libertasfilmfestival.com
The Procession of the Religious Brotherhoods (Good Friday –
6 Apr 2012; 29 Mar 2013) More ceremonial than religious these
days, but a riot of pomp (and more dressing up). ❸ Korčula

June–September
The Moreška Sword Dance A tradition that's evolved into a major
tourist draw for Korčula. ❸ Trg Sv Marka, Korčula Ⓒ 21.00 Thur (June
& Sept); 21.00 Mon & Thur (July & Aug)

July
Dalmatian Klapa Festival Klapa is a form of traditional, unaccompanied
folk singing that's enjoying a huge renaissance in Croatia. Various
festivals are held each July, the most famous one in Omiš near Split.
❸ Omiš Ⓦ www.fdk.hr (Croatian only)

July & August
Dubrovnik Summer Festival (mid-July–mid-Aug) This highly acclaimed
international festival hosts everything from ballet to Shakespeare.
Performances take place in the squares and courtyards of the
Old Town (see page 14). Ⓦ www.dubrovnik-festival.hr

SAINT BLAISE: THE PATRON SAINT OF DUBROVNIK

If you feel that eyes are watching you as you walk around Dubrovnik, they are likely to be those of Sv Vlaho (St Blaise), whose image seems to be everywhere. He is the symbol of the Dubrovnik Republic and appears on the state flag and coins, on the cannons that were once placed along the city walls and over gateways into the city. Historically, St Blaise was a 4th-century physician and spiritual leader who, according to legend, saved the life of a child who was choking to death on a fish bone. He thus became the patron saint of people with ailments, particularly sore throats.

While a bishop, in AD 316, St Blaise became caught up in a sporadic anti-Christian campaign that was being waged by the Roman emperor Diocletian (even though the Edict of Milan, passed three years earlier, was supposed to allow Christians the freedom to practise their religion officially). No one is quite sure how he was martyred, but one account claims he was flayed to death with iron combs, which is why a comb is often used as his emblem; he is also the patron saint of wool-combers.

Four centuries after his death, a cathedral priest dreamt that St Blaise had appeared to him, telling him that a fleet of Venetian galleons was anchored off the island of Lokrum near Dubrovnik and pretending to take on water barrels; in reality it was preparing to attack. The priest warned the officials, saved the city, and St Blaise was officially made Dubrovnik's patron saint in 972. St Blaise is celebrated annually on 3 February with holy services and a parade of his relics around the town.

◆ *St Blaise: Dubrovnik's patron saint*

⬤ *Fireworks sparkle behind the cathedral tower of St Domnius in Split*

August
Ladja Marathon (second Sat in Aug) A *ladja* is a type of ancient canoe, and every year over 30 teams of 12 people row a race on a 22.5-km (14-mile) route from Metković to Ploče. Around 50,000 fans line the banks of the River Neretva to enjoy the spectacle.

September
Julian Rachlin & Friends Festival In 2000, Lithuanian master violinist Julian Rachlin fell in love with Dubrovnik during the Summer

Festival. Every September he invites soloists and orchestras from across the world to play beautiful classical chamber music for 12 days, with the city squares as his concert hall. Ⓦ www.rachlin andfriends.com

September & October
Festival of New Film & Video (mid-Sept) A highly regarded festival that features independent short films from Croatia and full-length foreign releases. ❸ Split Ⓦ www.splitfilmfestival.hr

December
New Year's Eve Celebrations Both Dubrovnik and Split see the New Year in with a bang, with street concerts, fireworks and widespread partying – not one for the lily-livered.

PUBLIC HOLIDAYS
New Year's Day 1 Jan
Epiphany 6 Jan
Easter Sunday 8 April 2012, 31 March 2013, 20 April 2014
Easter Monday 9 April 2012, 1 April 2013, 21 April 2014
International Worker's Day 1 May
Corpus Christi 7 June 2012, 30 May 2013, 19 June 2014
Anti-Fascist Resistance Day 22 June
Croatian National Day (Statehood Day) 25 June
Feast of the Assumption 15 August
All Saints' Day 1 November
Christmas Day 25 December
St Stephen's Day 26 December

Dubrovnik Summer Festival

The Dubrovnik Summer Festival is the big one: Dubrovnik's most important cultural festival of the year, bar none. Attracting an international line-up of artists, it's the biggest and best festival, not only in Dubrovnik, but in all of Croatia. Over the years, it has attracted such celebrated names as Herbert von Karajan, Yehudi Menuhin, Zubin Mehta, Monserrat Caballe, Isaac Stern and the Vienna Boys' Choir. Don't expect to see the likes of Take That, though – the Dubrovnik Summer Festival celebrates ballet, opera and jazz (stars like Duke Ellington and Dizzy Gillespie have played here).

The festival was born in September 1950 during a period when many theatrical and musical events were springing up all over Europe. Kicking off mid-July, the 45-day festival makes use of every available space in town for a long list of concerts and theatrical performances that take place in every courtyard, square and bastion. In 1952, Marko Fotez, one of the original group of enthusiasts who started the festival, brought a production of *Hamlet* to the Lovrijenac Fort, and this soon became the favoured setting for the famous Shakespearean classic. Some of the Renaissance-Baroque architecture of the town has, over the years, provided equally appropriate backdrops for many classic works such as Goethe's *Iphigenia*, which was staged by the great Croatian director Branko Gavella, and Vojnović's *The Trilogy of Dubrovnik*, set in the authentic rooms of the Knežev dvor (Rector's Palace, see page 63). And dance companies such as Alvin Ailey, Merce Cunningham and Martha Graham have set their pieces in historic locations.

Tickets for the headliner events usually sell out well in advance, so anyone planning to attend should check out the festival website (Ⓦ www.dubrovnik-festival.hr) as soon as the programme becomes available, usually in April. Tickets are available online as well as at the festival kiosks on Stradun (see page 64), at the tourist information offices and at some hotels. It's also a good idea to book accommodation very early since the town fills up quickly at festival time. For more information, phone ☎ (020) 326 100 or email ✉ info@dubrovnik-festival.hr

🔺 *Numerous concerts take place around the city during the Summer Festival*

History

If Dubrovnik knows one thing well, it is that beauty has its price. Almost from its founding in the 7th century, Dubrovnik (formerly known as Ragusa) has been forced to pay off potential conquerors – and indeed continued to do so right up to the 20th century – in order to preserve its internal autonomy or save the city from destruction. Byzantine emperors, Venetian doges, Normans, Hungarians, Turks – all demanded tribute as a price of leaving Dubrovnik alone.

By the 15th and 16th centuries, Dubrovnik was experiencing a Golden Age with a merchant fleet that ranked third in the world and a ruling class that spent lavishly on the arts. However, when the great earthquake of 1667 either destroyed or damaged every building in the city, Dubrovnik was already experiencing a downturn; by now England and Holland dominated the seas and trade had shifted to the Americas. There was chaos after the quake as people fled in panic rather than trying to control fires. When the city was finally rebuilt, it was in the white stone that dominates today rather than the elaborately wealthy Renaissance style of before. For the next two centuries Dubrovnik was caught between adversaries, as the Habsburg Empire battled with the Turks and Napoleon with Russia, each empire crashing in its turn.

When the Habsburg Empire was finally pulled apart in 1918, Dubrovnik was incorporated into the newly created Yugoslavia. This hobbled along through recessions and hardships until World War II, when Communist partisans became the only effective force against the Axis occupation. After Dubrovnik was liberated in 1944, it became part of the Republic of Croatia, a semi-autonomous unit within Yugoslavia under Marshal Tito. Here it remained until the final collapse of Communism in 1989.

In 1991, with the United States refusing to recognise Croatian independence and Serbia pushing for a unified Yugoslavia, war once again broke out. The Yugoslav army began its attack on Dubrovnik on 1 October, overrunning tourist resorts in the south, shelling targets within the city and destroying the airport and the seaport at Gruž. The bombardment lasted until May 1992 when finally, once again, Dubrovnik's beauty saved the day. Since the city had been declared a UNESCO World Heritage Site and its city walls recognised as Europe's best, there was a huge global outcry at this terrible destruction. The attacking forces retreated, but they left behind a city with almost all of its hotels damaged in one way or another, and much of the rest scarred from mortars or shelling.

Dubrovnik has recovered well. The city authorities have been whittling away at the immense debt incurred from the war and by 2007 all damaged buildings were repaired. With the recent reopening of the cable car to the top of Mount Srđ, Dubrovnik is clearly back in business.

◓ *The new cable car with the city and Lokrum Island below*

Lifestyle

Croats see themselves as belonging to the Western world, even though in terms of religion the country stands between Islam and Orthodox Christianity in the East and the Catholicism of central Europe. The official language, according to the constitution, is Croat, but in the large cities and along the coast most people speak at least one foreign language (usually English, though this is sometimes complemented by German and/or Italian).

When meeting a Croatian, it's usual to shake hands, although a kiss on the cheek is appropriate when it's a friend. Croatians tend to be friendly but not obsequious – shopkeepers and waiters are not universally helpful. In conversations, tread carefully when the 1991 war comes up: it can be a conversational minefield, since years of intermarriage have blurred any clear dividing lines between Serb and Croat. The country's cultural heritage is a safe subject that will make you friends.

As a visitor, casual clothing when sightseeing and on the beach is usual, but churches frown on anything scanty – legs and shoulders should be covered (this is not a rule, but will save embarrassment). For business, appearance is important: this means a suit and tie for men and business dress for women. Restaurants and nightclubs don't require this kind of formality, but Croatians always try to look their best when going out. One place where you don't have to worry about dress is at one of the many nudist beaches (these have signs with the letters FKK on them). At family beaches, it is OK to go topless, except when going into a beachside bar or restaurant, when tops should be worn.

When it comes to food, Croatians usually eat lunch relatively late in the afternoon, so restaurants have a kind of daily brunch called

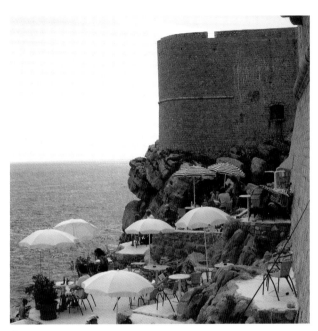

🔺 *Have a drink and a swim from the rocks at Buza café*

marende that's available in the morning. (It's similar to lunch, but with smaller portions.) Pizzerias, perhaps a legacy from the years of Venetian rule, are everywhere, and no Croatian town is without one. Another inheritance, this time from Habsburg rule, is a love of pastries. Local *slastičarnice* (patisseries) are filled with tortes and rolls and lots of goodies stuffed with whipped cream. At mealtimes, Croatians usually clink glasses and look directly into each other's eyes while cooing *Živjeli* (which translates as 'All the very best').

Culture

Having experienced hundreds of years of foreign occupation, Croatia has a rich and multifaceted cultural heritage that has left Greek and Roman ruins covered up by later layers of Venetian Gothic and Habsburg splendour. This influence is seen clearly in the architecture and cathedrals, particularly in the work of such sculptors as Juraj Dalmatinac of Zadar in the 15th century. Dalmatian artists worked closely with Italian artists, adopting the Italian Renaissance style, and much of their work sits today in international museums. Also of Dalmatian origin was the 20th-century sculptor Ivan Meštrović, whose simple, emotionally powerful work won him many admirers, including Rodin. A large collection of his sculptures can be seen at his former home in Zagreb.

Croatian literature, like its art, was strongly influenced by the Italian Renaissance and flowered in the Dalmatian region. One of Dubrovnik's most famous writers, Ivan Gundulić, was born in the late 16th century. He is considered Croatia's greatest poet. His epic poem, *Osman*, which celebrates the Polish victory over the Turks in 1621, is a Croatian classic. The plays of 16th-century playwright Marin Držić (after whom the theatre in Dubrovnik is named, see page 32) are still performed and enjoyed today. Among more contemporary writers, Miroslav Krleža is a giant, a novelist and playwright whose books have been translated into English. Ivo Andrić, born in Bosnia of Croatian parents, won the Nobel Prize for Literature in 1961 for his work, which includes *The Bridge on the Drina* (1945).

Dubrovnik's annual highlight is the **Summer Festival** (see page 14), when the whole town becomes a stage. International figures in the worlds of opera and music come to perform at the 45-day festival that culminates in a huge fireworks display. The cultural scene for

◆ *The Marin Držić Theatre*

● *Traditional folk dancing and music in Čilipi*

the rest of 'the season' (roughly May to October) is equally rich: Dubrovnik has its own symphony orchestra, theatre groups and dance ensembles. The indefatigable symphony performs year-round in a number of venues, such as the Revelin Fortress (see page 32), just outside the Ploče Gate, and the Sv Spasa (St Saviour's Church, see page 58) on Stradun, just inside the Pile Gate. Throughout the summer there are impromptu open-air rock and jazz performances.

Folk dancing and folk music are tremendously popular with young and old alike. The massive popularity of the **LADO Ensemble** (Ⓦ www.lado.hr), a folk collective who turns up every year at the Summer Festival and routinely brings the house down, shows that traditional culture is of huge importance to Croatians. Dubrovnik is also home to one of the country's most famous folk troupes – the 300-strong **Linđo Ensemble** (Ⓦ www.lindjo.hr).

● *The Cathedral's Baroque dome from the Romanesque cloister*

MAKING THE MOST OF
Dubrovnik

Shopping

As a shopping destination, Croatia is not the trendiest place, but it does produce some interesting items that are good to take home as gifts or for your store-cupboard. Croatia has had a long tradition of skilled handicraft production, the best examples of which tend to be lacework and embroidery. The latter is found almost everywhere; a characteristic design is red stitching on a white background, used on table linens, pillowcases and blouses. Pag lace (see page 135) is the most famous in the country, and is made using skills dating back to the Renaissance.

● *The farmers' market in Dubrovnik offers delicious local produce*

TIE ONE ON

Of all the millions of businessmen who knot their ties each morning, few realise that the wearing of a tie actually began in Croatia. It all started in the early 17th century, when Croatian soldiers started wearing narrow scarves tied loosely around the neck. When foreign soldiers came to Paris during the Thirty Years War, among them were Croatian mercenaries who were wearing their scarves. The Croatians' stylish neckties impressed the French, always on the lookout for a fashion statement, so by 1650 neckwear *la croate* had hit the court of Louis XIV. This phrase evolved into *la cravate*. Not long after, King Charles II, in exile in France, fell in love with the style. When he returned to England he took it with him as the height of culture and elegance.

Two shopping centres have sprung up near the harbour at Gruž, **Shopping Centar MINČETA** (❷ Nikole Tesle 2 ❾ www.minceta.hr) and **Shopping Centar Srd** (❷ Obala Stjepana Radića 25). Neither presents any radical retail revelations, but they can be useful.

Local food and drink products will be high on most shoppers' lists. The local variety of olive oil can be bought all over the city, and when it's mixed with herbs it makes a fabulous present (or medicine!). Lavender and other herbs made into fragrant oils or bound into sachets make a good and inexpensive gift. Some of the best lavender products come from the island of Hvar (see page 126). Another good (if heavy) gift are the stone products from the island of Brač, which are usually in the form of candlesticks, ashtrays or vases. Penkala writing instruments (named after Slavoljub Eduard Penkala, the Croatian inventor of the

USEFUL SHOPPING PHRASES

What time do the shops open/close?
Koliko je zatvaraju otvaraju/trgovine?
`Ko-li-ko ye `zat-va-ra-yoo ot-va-ra-yoo/tr-`go-vine?

How much is this?
Koliko to košta?
`Ko-li-ko to kohr-shta?

Can I try this on?
Mogu li to probati?
Mo-goo li to `pro-ba-ti?

My size is ...
Moj broj je ...
Moy broy ye ...

I'll take this one, thank you
Hvala, uzet ću ovo
Hva-la, oo-zet choo o-vo

This is too large/too small/too expensive.
Do you have any others?
Ovo je preveliko/premalo/preskupo. Imate li nešto drugo?
O-vo ye `pre-ve-li-ko/`pre-ma-lo/`pre-skoo-po. `I-ma-te li ne-shto droo-go?

first mechanical pencil and the first solid-ink fountain pen) can be found in most stationery stores and tourist shops, as can ties and cravats – Croatia just happens to be their birthplace (see page 25).

Some of the best souvenirs tend to be edible or drinkable, particularly wines and speciality liqueurs such as Bremet liquor or brandies with herbs in the bottles. Croatian wines are not well known abroad, mainly because they are produced in such small quantities, but they are surprisingly good, as is *rakija*, a distilled spirit made from a grape base that is normally drunk as an aperitif or digestif. Among the white wines, good choices are Pošip and Grk (from Korčula, see page 76), Vugava, Malvazija and Traminac. For reds, try the Dingač, Plavac and Babić.

Cheeses are excellent, particularly those from the island of Pag, or goat's cheese from Lika, but be sure to eat them before you return or buy sealed packages to avoid confiscation at customs. Croatian *tartufi* (truffles) and truffle-based products (like oils) are a good buy, as are herbal teas, which are usually available freshly dried in the markets. Do buy some onions – the sweet, sweet onions of Croatia are a very special treat. *Ajvar* is another taste sensation: a red, creamy paste made of ripe red peppers that is wonderful on sandwiches or with cold cuts. You can buy it in jars. For the sweet tooth, *paprenjak* is a traditional aromatic pastry made of honey, walnuts and pepper that even comes in specially designed boxes or bags.

⬥ *Croatian cloth of varied colours is a typical souvenir*

Eating & drinking

When it's mealtime, look for a *restoran*, *restauracija* or *konoba* (tavern). A *gostiona* (inn) is a more basic version of a *restoran*. For Croatians, the most important meal of the day is *ručak* (lunch), which they eat relatively late in the afternoon. For visitors, lighter meals (low-cost, small portions) are available during the *marende*, a kind of brunch snack.

For a picnic lunch, the nearest open-air market or *samoposluga* (supermarket) will carry the bread, cheese, meats, fruit and vegetables that you need. Bread can be bought at a *pekarnica* (bakery) and sandwiches can often be made up on request. *Lisnato tijesto* is puff pastry filled with cheese, meat or vegetables. *Burek* (a pie filled with meat or cheese) and *ćevapčići* (grilled 'kebabs' served in a flat bread bun called *somun*) make a quick, tasty snack.

In Dubrovnik, and all along the Dalmatian coast, plain, grilled seafood dishes are the big favourite; all are seasonal and supremely fresh. The classic is grilled fish served with olive oil and lemon with *blitva sa krumpirom* (swiss chard and potatoes with garlic and olive oil) as an accompaniment. Another favourite is shellfish *na buzaru* (quickly cooked with white wine, garlic and parsley). Shellfish not to miss here are *ostrige* (oysters) and *dagnje* (mussels).

Croatians like to serve their cheese first, before the main meal, often with *pršut*, a home-cured ham from Istria or Dalmatia, and

PRICE CATEGORIES

Price ratings are for a basic meal of main course, salad and a drink.

£ under 100kn   **££** 100–150kn   **£££** over 150kn

🔺 *Enjoy the café culture of Split*

olives. This typical and delicious delicacy goes through a long process of cleaning, salting, hanging and smoking; it will melt in your mouth. *Paški sir* comes from the island of Pag (see page 134) and is a hard, piquant cheese that has a taste somewhere between Parmesan and mature cheddar. Soups are usually clear and light and served with very thin noodles.

For main courses, grilled or pan-fried chops are popular, and come either plain or as a *bečki odrezak* (schnitzel), or *Zagrebački odrazak* (stuffed with cheese and ham). *Mješano meso* (mixed grill) is on most menus and consists of pork or veal cutlet, a few rissoles of minced meat and perhaps some spicy *kobasica* (sausage). Lamb is often prepared as a spit-roast; you can sometimes see a whole lamb being cooked beside the restaurant. Stews reflect the central European heritage, with *gulaš* (goulash) done as a sauce over pasta and *pašticada* (beef in vinegar, wine and prunes). Italian-influenced risottos are a popular accompaniment to the main course, especially 'black risotto', made with squid ink.

For dessert, try a Dubrovnik speciality called *rožata*, the local crème caramel. Other typical desserts include *sladoled* (ice cream), *torta* (cake) and *palačinke* (thin pancakes, which are usually filled with marmalade, walnuts with cream or chocolate sauce).

Most restaurants serve wine by the glass, carafe or bottle, while *kavanas* have a full range of alcoholic and non-alcoholic drinks as well as pastries and ice creams. A *kafić* is a smaller version of a *kavana* and usually caters to a younger crowd. Cafés and café-bars open early for that mandatory morning espresso and start serving alcohol from 09.00. The usual closing time is 23.00, although they sometimes stay open later in the summer.

Pubs tend to look a bit British; they serve both local and imported beers. Croatian beers are usually high quality – some good local brands are Ožujsko and Karlovačko, or Tomislav, which is a domestic dark beer. Croatian wines, both red and white, are good, with the best of them being from the Pelješac Peninsula or from Korčula (try the fruity dry whites from Pošip and Grk). *Prošek* is a sweet wine, tawny red in colour, which is usually chilled with an ice cube or two. *Travarica* is a strong grappa flavoured with herbs, *lozovača* is grappa made from grapes, while *šljivovica* (brandy) is made from plums.

Service charges aren't usually included in the bill, so the common practice (as when paying for a taxi too) is to round up the bill to the nearest 10 kuna or up to 10 per cent on bigger bills. If the service has not been good, then it's up to you whether you tip or not.

USEFUL DINING PHRASES

I would like a table for ... people
Trebam stol za .... osoba
Tre-bam stol za ... `o-so-ba

May I have the bill, please?
Platiti, molim?
`Pla-ti-ti, mo-lim?

Waiter!/Waitress!
Konobar!/Konobarica!
Ko-no-bar!/Ko-no-ba-ri-tsa!

Could I have it well cooked/medium/rare, please?
Molim vas, za mene dobro pečeno/polupečeno/
na engleski način?
*Mo-lim vas, za me-ne do-bro pe-che-no/`po-loo-pe-che-no/
na `en-gle-ski na-chin?*

I am a vegetarian. Does this contain meat?
Ja sam vegetarijanac. Da li ovo ima mesa?
Ya sam ve-ge-ta-ri-ya-nats. Da li o-vo ima me-sa?

Where is the toilet (restroom) please?
Molim vas, gdje je WC?
Mo-lim vas, gdie ye ve tse?

I would like a cup of/two cups of/another coffee/tea
Molim jednu/dvije/još jednu kavu/jedan/dva/još jedan čaj
*Mo-lim yed-noo/dvie/yosh yed-noo ka-voo/ye-dan/dva/
yosh ye-dan chay*

Entertainment & nightlife

The big entertainment events are staged in the warm summer months, the most notable being the huge Dubrovnik Summer Festival (see page 14). Adding to the rich cultural environment, there are informal open-air pop and jazz concerts in the Old Town during the high season, and special events at the town's two main cultural institutions – the **Marin Držić Theatre** (❷ Pred Dvorom 3 ❶ (020) 322 149), which specialises in serious drama (Croatian), and the **Dubrovnik Symphony**, which holds concerts year-round at the Knežev dvor (Rector's Palace, see page 63). The grounds of the Revelin Fortress just outside the Ploče Gate are another popular venue. (For all details, contact the tourist information office – see page 152.) Tickets for the symphony can be bought from the DSO office on ❷ Ulica Sv Dominika 9 or via ❿ www.dso.hr

The **Kino Sloboda** (❷ Luža bb ❶ (020) 321 425) is the city's main cinema. Most films are subtitled rather than dubbed into Croatian, and tickets are cheap. However, make sure you look for films made in English-speaking countries, or you may find yourself listening to characters speaking Russian with Croatian subtitles.

The best selection of bars is in the Old Town, with many of them prominent on the popular marbled streets. Wander down some of the labyrinthine alleys to find not only some of the more interesting and less typical bars but also the less crowded and less expensive. The Old Town is lively at night with lots of live music played in the cafés, especially during the summer season, but actual 'nightlife' is a bit thinner on the ground. **Club Lazareti** (❷ Frana Supila 8 ❶ (020) 324 633 ❿ www.arl.hr), out past the Ploče Gate, has the hippest music, DJs and dancing – they occasionally organise live rock, jazz and ethno gigs as well. There are discos in most major hotels during the summer months, while some city clubs transfer to the open air at coastal resorts during the summer. There's not much information in the local press on events, so the best bet is to ask around or look for posters in town.

⬥ There are plenty of bars and restaurants in the Old Town

Sport & relaxation

SPECTATOR SPORTS
Football
As in the rest of Croatia, *nogomet* (football) is keenly followed in Dubrovnik. There's a local team called **NK Gošk**, which was put together by a Dubrovnik entrepreneur. They usually play in the Gradksi Stadion Lapad (1 km/²/₃ mile northwest of the city centre).

Water polo
Water polo is the number-one sport in Dubrovnik, and watching **VK Jug** (ⓦ www.jug.hr), one of the world's best water-polo clubs, is a very popular pastime among Croatians. A league called **Divlja Liga** (ⓦ www.divjaliga.hr) plays during the summer, with each team representing one of Dubrovnik's beaches. Half-serious, half-fun, this is for amateurs only and everyone can join in. If you want to play, contact the attendants on your beach.

PARTICIPATION SPORTS
Climbing
With a long climbing tradition, Croatia was one of the first nations in the world to found a national climbing organisation. For information on where to climb, contact the **Croatian Climbing Federation** (ⓐ Kozarčeva 22, Zagreb ⓣ (01) 482 41 42).

Extreme sports
Try paintball, or even bungee-jumping from the elegant Franjo Tuđman suspension bridge. You don't have to book a jump, just turn up any time between 1 May and 1 October. It's near the modern port, west of the Old Town in the suburb of Gruž.

Hiking

Hiking is one of the best ways of seeing the beautiful countryside around Dubrovnik. The path above Šipčine will take you up to the top of Mount Srđ for an amazing view of the archipelago. Other good hikes include several at Župa and on the Pelješac Peninsula.

Horse riding

On a sunny day, with the ocean breezes blowing, the place to be is in Konavle (to the south), where they have a number of small horse ranches. The **Kojan Koral Riding Center** (ⓐ Popovići, Kokoti 3, Gruda ⓘ (098) 606 929, ask for Pero Kojan Ⓦ www. kojankoral.hr) organises five-hour treks along the Adriatic coastline.

Watersports

With great lakes and warm coastal water, watersports are big in Croatia – windsurfing, fishing, scuba diving (see page 103), sailing, rowing, water polo and kayaking. A number of companies, such as **Aurora Maris** (ⓐ Sv Križa 3 ⓘ (020) 313 444 Ⓦ www.auroramaris. com), have fleets of charter boats for bareboat or skippered sailing. For detailed information, contact the tourist office (see page 152). For fishermen, there's everything from big-game fishing to fly fishing, but a licence is required. For details, call the **Ministry of Agriculture** (ⓐ Marka Majorice 4 ⓘ (020) 332 393).

RELAXATION

There are two fitness centres in Dubrovnik:
Fiziofitness Lapad ⓐ Kardinala Stepinca 18 ⓘ (020) 436 899
Ⓝ Bus: line 5
Wellness Dalmacija ⓐ Grand Villa Argentina, Frana Supila 14
ⓘ (020) 440 596 Ⓝ Bus: line 8

Accommodation

Dubrovnik has been in the hotel business in one form or another since 1347, and has survived through many vicissitudes. During the siege of Dubrovnik, however, the city lost around half of its hotel availability. Thankfully, the accommodation situation is improving fast.

If you want to stay right in the city centre, there is not a massive choice. There are excellent options outside the Old Town, though, and these are at most a short walk or bus ride away from the centre. If money is no object, there are some great places overlooking the sea just east of the town walls; while in the mid-range there are a number of options on the Lapad Peninsula, about 3 km (nearly 2 miles) from the centre, or in the Gruž port area. If you have access to a car, you can look at some of the pension-style places in the villages around Dubrovnik.

During the summer season, there's a big demand for rooms, especially by tour groups who block-book, so independent travellers should book well in advance. Prices in the highest season (July and August) can be 20 per cent or more higher than winter or off-season rates.

A word of warning: anyone arriving via ferry or bus is likely to be swamped with offers of unlicensed rooms, and while some of these

PRICE CATEGORIES

Gradings used in this book are based on cost per person for two people sharing the least expensive double room with en-suite bathroom and breakfast in high season (July & August).

£ under 750kn   ££ 750–1,500kn   £££ over 1,500kn

may turn out to be OK, others may be a long way from the centre
of town and have all sorts of hidden 'extra costs' associated –
so be careful.

HOTELS

Argosy £ Situated in the heavenly oasis of Babin Kuk, we're talking
greenery, we're talking fragrant, we're talking great value. Good for
children. ⓐ Iva Dulčića 41 ⓣ (020) 446 100 ⓦ www.valamar.com
ⓝ Bus: line 7 from Gruž or 5 and 6 from Pile

🔺 *The charming Hilton Imperial (see page 40)*

Lapad £ Once a graceful summer villa, this large hotel has good basic rooms and public areas that echo its former life. Small swimming pool. ⓐ Lapadska obala 37 ⓣ (020) 432 922 ⓦ www.hotel-lapad.hr ⓝ Bus: line 9 and 6 from Pile

Neptun £ On the Babin Kuk, this ten-storey building has south-facing rooms, most with a sea view. Its bright, self-contained, airy rooms are good for families. Near the beach. ⓐ Kardinala Stepinca 31 ⓣ (020) 440 100 ⓦ www.importanneresort.com ⓝ Bus: line 5 from Pile

Zagreb £ Great value in this small 2-star hotel with clean rooms in a lovely old building. ⓐ Šetalište Kralja Zvonimira 27, Lapad ⓣ (020) 438 930 ⓝ Bus: line 6 from Pile or 7 from Gruž

The Berkeley ££ A family-owned hotel that offers 24 rooms and apartments. Excellent. ⓐ Ulica Andrije Hebranga 116A ⓣ (020) 494 160 ⓦ www.berkeleyhotel.hr ⓝ Bus: line 8 from Pile

Dubrovnik ££ A 3-star hotel by the beach in Uvala Lapad, just 7 km (4^1/$_3$ miles) from the Old Town. Has its own tennis courts. ⓐ Šetalište Kralja Zvonimira bb ⓣ (020) 435 030 ⓦ www.hotel dubrovnik.hr ⓝ Bus: line 7 from Gruž or 6 from Pile

Stari Grad ££ This charming little hotel within the city walls has only eight rooms, but it also has a superb upper terrace where you can eat your breakfast while enjoying panoramic views over the bay. ⓐ Od Sigurate 4 ⓣ (020) 322 224 ⓦ www.hotelstarigrad.com

Villa Wolff ££ A first-class beach hotel in the Bay of Uvala Lapad, ten minutes by car from the city walls, it combines the comfort of a

hotel stay with the peace of a private residence. ⓐ Nika i Meda
Pucića 1 ① (020) 356 432 ⓦ www.villa-wolff.hr ⓝ Bus: line 4 from Pile

Bellevue £££ Located atop a cliff overlooking the Adriatic, this
modern five-storey property is situated just 800 metres (nearly
$1/2$ mile) from the city centre. ⓐ Pera Čingrije 7 ① (020) 330 000
ⓦ www.hotel-bellevue.hr ⓝ Bus: line 4 from Pile

Excelsior £££ A 5-star hotel with all the trimmings, fabulous views
and balconies facing the sea. ⓐ Frana Supila 12 ① (020) 353 353
ⓦ www.alh.hr

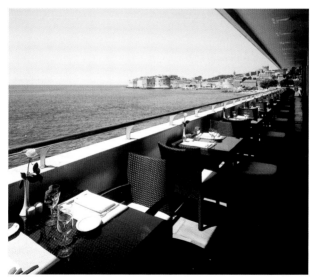

⬥ The Excelsior's magnificent sea view

Grand Villa Argentina £££ This is another rejuvenated 5-star hotel, with a swimming pool and beach area, several restaurants, a day spa and gym. It has fine views towards Dubrovnik Old Town and is within walking distance of the centre. ⓐ Frana Supila 14 ❶ (020) 440 555 ⓦ www.gva.hr

Hilton Imperial £££ Just a few steps away from the Pile Gate, this 5-star hotel, which was created out of two 19th-century palaces, has all the comforts you could wish for (including an indoor swimming pool) and an intriguing history: George Bernard Shaw and H G Wells stayed here. ⓐ Marijana Blažića 2, near Old Town ❶ (020) 320 320 ⓦ www.hilton.co.uk/dubrovnik

Pucić Palace £££ Once an 18th-century palace, this is now a 5-star hotel standing right on the main market square within the city walls. Plush and fully equipped. ⓐ Od Puča 1 ❶ (020) 326 222 ⓦ www.thepucicpalace.com

YOUTH HOSTELS
Dubrovnik Youth Hostel £ Between Gruž and the Old Town, this hostel has bunk-bed accommodation in four- to six-person dormitories. Basic breakfast on the terrace or kitchen facilities, but call in advance because it books up quickly in the summer. ⓐ Just off Bana Jelačića at Vinka Sagrestana 3 ❶ (020) 423 241 ⓦ www.hfhs.hr ⓔ dubrovnik@hfhs.hr ⓝ Bus: line 7 from Gruž or 4 from Pile

PRIVATE ROOMS
There is a huge supply of private rooms in Dubrovnik, and these can offer very good value for money as a budget option if you want to stay right in the centre. Dubrovnik travel agencies can be contacted

by email to book a room, or you can check a number of online resources (try Ⓦ www.dubrovnik-apartments.com).

Orhan £ Eleven basic but spotless rooms just down the street from the owner's restaurant. Nice location in a quiet cove below a fortress. Ⓐ Od Tabakarije 1, under Old Town Ⓣ (020) 414 183

Dubrovnik Apartment £–££ Should you be seeking a room in a lovely stone house that's surrounded by a garden filled with flowers and is owned by a charming couple, no further need you look. Ⓐ Janjinska 14 Ⓣ (091) 507 1320 Ⓦ www.apartment dinkadubrovnik.com

Apartment Anuška ££ Situated on Lapad Peninsula, Anuška is minutes away from fab beaches, clean sea, beautiful walking areas and rich Mediterranean vegetation. Ⓐ Batala 1 Ⓣ (091) 507 1320 Ⓦ www.dubrovnikapartment-anuska.com Ⓝ Bus: line 6 from Pile

Apartments Within Medieval Walls ££ Not, perhaps, the snappiest of titles for four apartments in a building just inside the city walls, but the rooms are lovely. Ⓐ Bandureva 1 Ⓣ (020) 323 433 Ⓦ www.karmendu.com

CAMPSITES
Camping Solitudo The best (if the only) site in the area offers exposure to nature alongside 300 pitches, a pool, a restaurant and tennis courts. Ⓐ Vatroslava Lisinskog 17 Ⓣ (020) 448 686 Ⓦ www.camping-adriatic.com Ⓝ Bus: line 7 from Gruž or 5 from Pile

THE BEST OF DUBROVNIK

A break in Dubrovnik will soothe your senses. Here you can enjoy the beauty of an ancient walled city, the startlingly clear blue waters of the Adriatic, the taste of superb fresh seafood and the sound of silence.

TOP 10 ATTRACTIONS

- **The city walls** A stroll along this aerial promenade of Europe's best city walls guarantees panoramic views of the Adriatic and glimpses of the rooftops and alleyways of the town (see page 58).

- **Franjevački Samostan (Franciscan Monastery)** Home to Croatia's most beautiful medieval cloister, the friary also has a history as a pharmacy dating back nearly 700 years (see page 60).

- **Stradun** Head to the main street that's at the heart of action in Dubrovnik, and spend a morning window-shopping, sipping cappuccino, and watching the world stroll by (see page 64).

- **Mount Srđ** Enjoy stunning views of the city and the Dalmatian islands from the top of Mount Srđ, easily reached by cable car (see page 60).

- **Korčula** A verdant isle that provides a taste of traditional Croatian life and has an attractive town with Venetian flavour (see page 76).

- **Cavtat** Accessible via a glorious boat trip and once the ancient city of Epidaurum, this is now a charming, palm-fringed resort (see page 88).

- **The Old Port** You won't taste fresher fish anywhere than at a restaurant right next to the market (see page 72).

- **Mljet** Hop on a ferry and enjoy the peace and quiet of the vast national park (see page 98).

- **The Elaphite Islands** Among the Adriatic coast's beautiful sandy beaches, these have the cleanest and clearest water (see page 92).

- **The oysters of Mali Ston** For lovers of seafood, these little rascals are an unmissable treat (see page 106).

🔻 *The Rector's Palace, once the heart of the Ragusa Republic*

Suggested itineraries

HALF-DAY: DUBROVNIK IN A HURRY

With only half a day to spare, the best move is to start with one of Dubrovnik's key selling points: the walk around the city walls (see page 58). You'll get sea views to the island of Lokrum and a great cityscape of the Old Town. Take a look at the Vrata od Pila (Pile Gate, see page 64), and then relax on the terrace of one of the lovely cafés just outside. Visit the superb Katedrala (Cathedral, see page 62) and, if there's time, head down the Stradun to see Europe's oldest continuously operating pharmacy in the Franjevački Samostan (Franciscan Monastery, see page 60).

1 DAY: TIME TO SEE A LITTLE MORE

In addition to the sites suggested above, the Dominikanski Samostan (Dominican Monastery, see page 60), with its stunning Renaissance pieces, is highly recommended. A tour of the Stradun is also very enjoyable, with the Old Town's best historic sights, such as Velika Onofrijeva Fontana (Onofrio's Great Fountain, see page 64) and the Sinagoga (Synagogue, see page 46). St John's Fortress houses the Pomorski Muzej (Maritime Museum, see page 67), which gives an overview of Dubrovnik's seafaring past. If it's very hot, then why not take a taxi-boat to the island of Lokrum and enjoy an afternoon of relaxing on the beaches there or take the cable car to the top of Mount Srđ (see page 60) to enjoy the views and the cool breeze?

2–3 DAYS: TIME TO SEE MUCH MORE

After spending the first day in the Old Town, take a trip to the Elaphite Islands, a short ferry-ride from Dubrovnik. The islands were a popular summer retreat for Ragusan nobles, and hiking through the pine woods with the scent of rosemary and sage in the air is a real delight. The three principal islands in the group, Koločep, Lopud and Šipan, all have sleepy villages surrounded by olive groves and vineyards. Koločep has a good sandy beach for swimming. You can stay overnight here and explore all three islands, or spend the third day in Cavtat, a charming fishing village set in a stunning bay around 30-minutes' boat ride from Dubrovnik.

LONGER: ENJOYING DUBROVNIK TO THE FULL

With more time, a day or two on Korčula provides a stunning diversion. A lush island covered in vineyards and ancient buildings, Korčula was the birthplace of Marco Polo in 1254. A visit to Split is also recommended, to take in the Roman ruins and history. For seafood lovers, a stop in Ston to sample fresh oysters is also a must. Or you can visit the stunning Neretva Delta Nature Park (ⓦ www.neretva.info).

🔺 *Take some time to relax beside the clear waters of the Adriatic*

Something for nothing

In Dubrovnik, the best things in life really are free: the views, the architecture, the sheer beauty of the town itself. Churches, cathedrals and monasteries abound here and admission fees are usually nominal. Crkva Sv Vlaha (❸ Pred Dvorom 3), the Baroque church dedicated to the city's patron saint, St Blaise (see page 10), contains a statue of him holding an early model of the city. There's also a lone 15th-century Sinagoga (Synagogue) on Žudioska Street, the second oldest of its kind in Europe. It contains 17th-century furnishings, Torah scrolls and other artefacts from a once-flourishing Jewish community.

Indoor and outdoor markets are high on the 'free list', and Dubrovnik's two daily ones are always a big draw for photographers. The old market on Gundulićeva poljana has everything from vegetables and flowers to fish and lace, while the main city market caters largely for local people. Another good subject for holiday snaps are the fountains in the city – Velika Onofrijeva Fontana (Onofrio's Great Fountain, see page 64) and Mala Onofrijeva Fontana (Onofrio's Small Fountain, see page 65), plus a number of others.

What about testing your balance for free? Just outside the entrance to the Franjevački Samostan (Franciscan Monastery) cloister (see page 60), there's an unusual stone with a gargoyle face that sticks out from the main wall. The ritual is to stand face to wall on this stone, arms outstretched, for as long as possible without falling off.

If you need a break from history, pick up a picnic lunch and head for one of the beaches (like the pebbled Banje beach) for a day of romping in the Adriatic's crystal-clear waters.

The streets themselves offer no end of surprises: you can step out of a church like St Blaise's and find a troupe of entertainers giving a folkloric show, or turn a corner and discover a group of thespians in Renaissance costume shooting a television series. There are also performance spaces and galleries that feature local talent in the stone buildings and courtyards known as the *Lazareti* (once quarantine houses for travellers during the Renaissance).

⬥ *Magnificent Onofrio's Great Fountain*

When it rains

Even though Dubrovnik chalks up many sunny days, it does rain every once in a while, so it's a good idea to save leisurely inspections of the interiors of the city's many churches for a drizzly day. Crkva Sv Spasa (St Saviour's Church, see page 58) and the Katedrala (Cathedral of the Assumption, see page 62) were both built as 'thank-yous' – the former for deliverance from an earthquake and the latter for deliverance from a storm.

If it's pouring, you can devote plenty of time to discovering the Franjevački Samostan (Franciscan Monastery, see page 60), with its Romanesque cloister and arches topped with carved human heads and fantastic animals. And the pharmacy at the entrance of the monastery is actually one of Europe's most famous. Still functioning, it dates back to 1317 and calls itself the oldest pharmacy in Europe.

Damp days are also a good time to hit the galleries, and one very good one is **War Photo Limited** (ⓐ Antuninska 6 ⓣ (020) 322 166 ⓛ 09.00–21.00 daily (May–Sept); closed Oct–Apr ⓘ Admission charge), run by a former war photographer, Wade Goddard. The gallery specialises in first-rate temporary exhibitions of the world's greatest war photographers. It's not for the very young or the faint-hearted: War Photo Limited sees itself as an educator in the field of war photography, aiming to look at war 'as it is': raw, frightening and venal. There are several other galleries worth visiting during cloudbursts, including the Museum of Modern Art (see page 65), which features paintings and sculptures by some of Croatia's best artists.

The Palača Sponza (Sponza Palace, see page 63) is also an enjoyable rainy-day destination. Built in the 16th century, it was originally used as the custom house and mint, and stages interesting exhibitions.

Shopping for some Croatian delicacies is also a terrific way to while away any periods of rain.

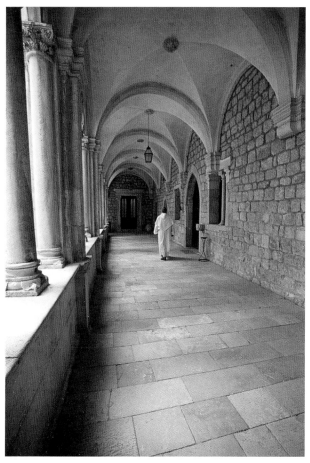

⬤ *The fine cloisters of the Franciscan Monastery*

On arrival

TIME DIFFERENCE

Croatia follows Central European Time (CET). During Daylight Saving Time (late Mar–late Oct), the clocks are put ahead one hour.

ARRIVING

By air

Most international flights end in Zagreb with a connection on to Dubrovnik. There are two or three flights a day between the cities and they take one hour. However, there are direct flights to Dubrovnik from the UK (see page 142). Dubrovnik Airport is around 20 km (12 miles) east of the city, close to the village of Čilipi. A Croatia Airlines airport bus makes regular runs to the city centre that take about 25 minutes, and taxi are also readily available – see ⓦ www.taxi-dubrovnik.hr for details ① 0800 09 70. Buses back to the airport leave the bus station 90 minutes before each Croatia Airlines departure. There is no tourist office in the airport, but there is a bank, post office, car-rental office and duty-free shop.
Dubrovnik Airport ① (020) 773 333 ⓦ www.airport-dubrovnik.hr

By rail

Perhaps rather surprisingly, Dubrovnik does not have a train station. The furthest towards the city that you can get by train is Split. From here, there are buses to Dubrovnik. See ⓦ www.croatiabus.hr for details.

By road

The bus station is in the port suburb of Gruž, 3 km (nearly 2 miles) west of the Old Town. Long-distance buses come straight to the bus station. There are two direct buses a day to/from Sarajevo, up to three to/from

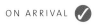

IF YOU GET LOST, TRY ...

Excuse me, do you speak English?
Oprostite, govorite li engleski?
O-`pro-sti-te, `go-vo-ri-te li `en-gle-ski?

**Can you tell me the way to the bus station/taxi rank/
city centre (downtown)/beach?**
Možete li mi reći kako mogu doći do autobusnog kolodvora/
taksi-stajalište/centra grada/plaže?
*`Mo-zhe-te li mi re-chi ka-ko mo-goo do-chi do`
`a-oo-to-boos-nog `ko-lo-dvo-ra/tak-si `sta-ya-li-shta/
tsen-tra gra-da/pla-zhe?

Can you point to it on my map?
Možete li mi to pokazati na planu grada?
`Mo-zhe-te li mi to po-`ka-za-ti na pla-noo gra-da?

Kotor and Budva, up to fifteen to/from Split and two per week to/from
Trieste. All buses south to Montenegro pass right by Dubrovnik Airport,
where there is a bus stop along the main road near the terminal.
Central Bus Station ⓐ Obala pape Ivana Pavla II 44A, Gruž ⓣ (060)
305 070 ⓦ www.libertasdubrovnik.hr ⓛ 05.30–22.30 daily
(May–Sept); 05.30–21.00 daily (Oct–Apr)

By water
The ferry terminal is just to the north of the bus station. Year-round,
overnight ferries depart weekly for Bari, Italy (see page 144).

ZAGREBAČKA

Buses to Cavtat

PLOČE

HVARSKA

UZ TABOR

Lower Cable-Car Station

M PERIĆA

FRANA SUPILA

ZA GRADA

Tvrđava Revelin

Dubrovnik ✈
Lazareti & Museum of Modern Art

City Walls

Vrata od Ploča

PELINE

Dominikanski Samostan

ZAMANJINA
DROPČEVA
BOŠKOVIĆEVA
ŽUDIOSKA
KOVAČKA
ZLATARSKA

PRIJEKO

SVETOG DOMINIKA

Rosarij

Kaše

Sinagoga i Židovski Muzej

Palača Sponza

OLD TOWN

RIBARNICA

Boats to Lokrum & Cavtat

Orlando's Column

LUŽA

Old Port

Clock Tower

IZMEĐU
USKA
POLAČA

Mala Onofrijeva Fontana

Lokrum & Cavtat

CVIJETE
ZUZORIĆ

Crkva Sv Vlaha

Marin Držić Theatre

OD
PUĆA
KABOGE

Knežev Dvor

Akvarij

USKA
MAROJICE
RANJINA
DINKA

GUNDULIĆEVA POLJANA

PRED DVOROM

PONTA

KNEZA DAMJANA JUDE

OD PUSTJERNE

STARA

Tvrđava Sv Ivana

UZ JEZUITE

BUNIĆEVA POLJANA

Katedrala ✝

DJBR
BRAĆE ANDRIĆA
RESTIĆEVA
BALBICA
POBJANA
SPOD MIRA

BANDUREVA

Pomorski Muzej

ANDROVIĆEVA

Jesuit Church

POLJANA R BOŠKOVIĆA

KNEZA HRVAŠA
VINTULIS
ILIJE
SARAKE

N

OD MARGARITE

FINDING YOUR FEET

Dubrovnik is compact and easy to navigate once you get a map and see the 'fish skeleton' layout of the streets. Walking around at night is pretty safe, and there's little overt crime. One obvious precaution is to lock up any valuable jewellery, rather than flaunting it on the streets.

The official language of the country is Croatian, but the majority of younger Croats speak fairly good English. Most people working in tourism will have a decent vocabulary, but it doesn't hurt to learn a few words. Croatians appreciate a visitor who makes the effort to communicate in the local language.

Women should note that Croatian men are quite open with their remarks. Most of these can simply be ignored, but if the man persists speak firmly and make your intentions to call for help clear. Drinking in public areas is fine, but there are bars patronised mainly by men, and these should be avoided: a woman alone gives off the wrong signals in these places.

● *Ferries link the islands to the mainland*

ORIENTATION

Tucked into its walls, Dubrovnik's Old Town is tiny, closed to traffic
and easy to navigate. To enter the city, there's a choice of three gates:
the Ponta Gate at the harbour entrance, the Vrata od Pila (Pile Gate,
see page 64) to the west, near the bus station, and the Ploče Gate to
the east. Each leads to the Stradun, the marbled 'main drag' that is
only 300 m (328 yds) in length and divides the Old Town. Narrow
staircases and alleys lead off the Stradun and it is buttressed by
two major parallel streets: Prijeko in the north and Od Puča in
the south.

Greater Dubrovnik spreads along the Dalmatian coast from the
suburb of Ploče in the southeast to the suspension bridge in the
northwest, and across the Lapad and Babin Kuk peninsulas to the west.
The main harbour, Gruž, sits between the mainland and Babin Kuk.
For maps and details, visit the tourist office (ⓐ Brsalje 5 ⓣ (020) 323
887 ⓦ www.tzdubrovnik.hr ⓛ 08.00–22.00 daily (summer);
08.00–16.00 Mon–Sat, closed Sun (winter)).

GETTING AROUND

On landing at Dubrovnik Airport (see page 50), there are two
ways to get into town, 20 km (12 miles) away. Atlas buses regularly
drive from the airport via the Old Town to the Central Bus Station
in Gruž. Buses to the airport depart from the Central Bus Station
(see page 51) 90 minutes before any Croatian Airlines flight and
two hours before other flights. Taxis cost around 200–250kn. For
passengers arriving by sea from the port of Gruž, buses (Nos 1A, 1B
and 3) run from the port to Pile Gate roughly every half-hour. The
No 8 bus runs from Ploče hotels to the Ploče Gate. Local buses cover
all of Dubrovnik and run from 04.30 until midnight (in summer until
02.30). Tickets are sold at newspaper kiosks or on the bus.

Dubrovnik has a good taxi service as well, with stands at the Pile Gate, Gruž, the bus station and Lapad. You can also get someone to call a taxi to pick up at any of the main hotels. As always, you should check to make sure the meter is turned on before you leave, unless you've pre-negotiated the fare to a particular destination.

To go to any of the islands, take one of the local ferries or a taxi-boat – these travel between Dubrovnik's old port and Lokrum every half-hour in the summer. It's a ten-minute crossing. There are also regular boats to and from Cavtat. All other ferries leave from the main quay on Gruž harbour and are usually operated by Jadrolinija, the national ferry company (see page 126).

Car hire

Hiring a car in Dubrovnik is expensive, at around 500kn a day for an economy car with unlimited mileage. Since the Old Town is so compact for sightseeing, it might not be advisable to rent unless you plan to do some extensive touring around – ferries and buses are a good alternative. The major hire companies have offices in Dubrovnik, but usually you get the best-value rates by booking at home before you leave, either through your airline or on the web. You can try these car-hire companies in the UK:

Autoeurope ☎ 0800 358 1229 Ⓦ www.auto-europe.co.uk

Budget ☎ 0844 544 3470 Ⓦ www.budget.co.uk

easyCar ☎ 08710 500 444 Ⓦ www.easycar.com

Europcar ☎ 08713 849 847 Ⓦ www.europcar.co.uk

Hertz ☎ 0870 844 8844 Ⓦ www.hertz.co.uk

⊙ *Aerial view of the Old Town and port*

THE CITY OF
Dubrovnik & around

Old Town

Dubrovnik's Old Town is compact and the main sights are close to one another, so that you can see them all without any lengthy stops within a couple of hours. If you have a special interest, say in Renaissance art or musical notation, and want to do a thorough exploration, you should allow at least a half a day.

SIGHTS & ATTRACTIONS

City walls

Depending on whom you talk to, Dubrovnik's city walls (in purple on the map opposite) are the most beautiful, best-preserved, or most complete city walls in the world. It's certainly the place to start any visit to the city. Wrapping themselves around Dubrovnik for just a little under 2 km (1^1/$_4$ miles), they measure 25 m (82 ft) at their highest point and 12 m (39 ft) at their widest.

The whole circuit can be done in a leisurely hour. Begun in the 8th century, building and repairing went on throughout the centuries, including the extensive work that was carried out on them after the 1991 war. There are three entrances on to the walls: one is next to Vrata od Pila (Pile Gate), another on Sv Dominika leading to the Dominikanski Samostan (Dominican Monastery) and the third on Kneza Damjana Jude near the **Akvarij** (Aquarium ❸ Kneza Damjana Jude 12 🕐 08.00–19.00 in the summer, with shorter hours in the winter).

Crkva Sv Spasa (St Saviour's Church)

Near Onofrio's Great Fountain, this church (see map page 52) was erected as the city's 'thank-you' for surviving the 1520 earthquake.

Old Town

- PELINE
- City Walls
- N
- PALMOTICEVA
- MEDOVICA
- CELESTINA
- SIGURATE
- OD
- PALMOTICEVA
- PRIJEKO
- ANTUNINSKA
- NALJESKOVICEVA
- KUNICEVA
- PETILOVRIJENCI
- VETRANICEVA
- ZAMANJINA
- DROPCEVA
- BOSKOVICEVA
- ZUDIOSKA
- KOVACKA
- PELINE
- PRIJEKO
- PESKARIJA
- Dominikanski Samostan
- Rosarij
- Palača Sponza
- ❷
- Franjevački Samostan
- War Photo Ltd ❶
- KUNICEVA
- VETRANICEVA
- Sinagoga i Židovski Muzej
- ❸
- ❿ ⓫
- STRADUN (PLACA)
- Orlando's Column
- LUŽA
- Clock tower
- M. CVTALICEVA
- CUBRANOVICEVA
- DORĐICEVA
- SIPOLA
- VARA
- ⓭
- ❹
- IZMEĐU POLAČA
- USKA
- CVIJETE
- ZUZORIĆ
- Crkva Sv Vlaha
- Mala Onofrijeva Fontana
- Marin Držić Theatre ❺
- OD
- PUCA
- Kuća Marina Držića
- Orthodox Church
- PRACATA
- BOŽIDAREVIĆA
- ❾
- Knežev Dvor
- PRED DVOROM
- ❼
- ZA ROKOM
- NIKOLE GUČETIĆA
- MIHA
- USKA
- MAROJICE
- KABOGE
- DINKA RANJINE
- OD PUCA
- GUNDULIĆEVA POLJANA
- Muzej Rupe
- DOMINA
- SV JOSIPA
- OD RUPA
- PEČARICA
- ❻
- UZ JEZUITE
- BUNIĆEVA POLJANA
- Katedrala ✝
- ❽
- SV MARIJE
- ZVIJEZDICEVA
- STROSMAJEROVA
- ANDROVIĆEVA
- Pomorski Muzej & Akvarij
- OD KASTELA
- SVETOG SIM
- CRIJEVIĆEVA
- Jesuit Church
- POLJANA R BOŠKOVIĆA
- KNEZA HRVAŠA
- STULINA
- City Walls
- OD MARGARITE
- ❷
- 0 ——— 50 metres
- 0 ——— 50 yards
- POI
- ✝ Cathedral
- ⓬

Dominikanski Samostan (Dominican Monastery)

This old structure, dating back to the early 14th century, has two attractions of major interest: its 15th-century Gothic-Renaissance cloister, filled with palm and orange trees, and its museum stuffed with a wealth of Renaissance treasures. Of historical interest, there's a painting of St Blaise holding a model of 16th-century, pre-quake Dubrovnik, a splendid Virgin and Child altarpiece, and a Titian altarpiece of Mary Magdalene and St Blaise. ⓐ Off Sv Dominika 4 ⓣ (020) 321 423 ⓛ 09.00–17.00 daily ⓘ Admission charge

Dubrovnik Cable Car

The newly reopened cable car (see map page 52) whisks visitors to the top of Mount Srđ in minutes, from where the views over the Old Town, the coast and the islands are magnificent. There's a restaurant, snack bar and viewing terraces by the old fortress at the top of the mountain. If you're energetic, it's also possible to walk along a path that hairpins steeply across the mountainside and then use the cable car. The cable-car station is just outside the Old Town walls. ⓐ Petra Krešimira ⓣ (020) 414 355 ⓦ www.dubrovnikcablecar.com ⓛ 09.00–20.00 daily (summer); 09.00–16.00 daily (winter) ⓘ Admission charge

Franjevački Samostan (Franciscan Monastery)

Beyond the peaceful and beautiful courtyard, the two most interesting parts of the monastery are the cloister and treasury. The capitals in the cloister are decorated with birds, animals and human faces, one of which is rumoured to be the sculptor suffering from a toothache. The frescoes in the cloister tell the life of St Francis. The friary is also notable for being the oldest continuously functioning pharmacy in Europe: it was founded in 1317. The treasury has relics from the ancient apothecary's shop as well as manuscripts tracing the history of musical

⬥ *The city was rebuilt with white limestone*

notation. Check out the 'balancing stone' beside the west portal.

ⓐ Placa 2 ⓣ (020) 321 410 ⓦ www.malabraca.hr ⓛ 09.00–18.00 daily (summer); 09.00–17.00 daily (winter)

Katedrala (Cathedral of the Assumption)

Located right in the heart of the city, the original cathedral was financed, according to legend, by Richard the Lionheart, after he survived a terrible storm just off the coast near Lokrum. At the height of the storm, the king vowed that – if he survived – he would build a church. Enterprising Ragusan nobles, on hearing of the pledge, sent a delegation to Richard, persuading the king that his money would best be used to build a church in Dubrovnik rather than Lokrum.

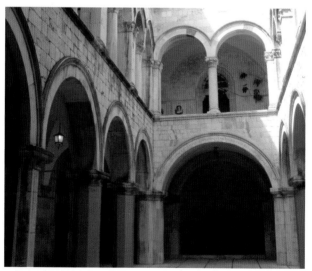

◔ The courtyard of Sponza Palace

🅐 Kneza Damjana Jude 1 ❶ (020) 323 459 🕐 09.00–17.00 Mon–Sat, 11.00–17.00 Sun (summer); 09.00–12.00, 15.00–17.00 Mon–Sat, 11.00–12.00 Sun (winter)

Knežev Dvor (Rector's Palace)

Twice blown up by gunpowder stored next door, this version of the palace dates to the 15th century and once housed all the major offices of state plus a dungeon (and the gunpowder storage). At the entrance, you walk through pillars made of Korčula marble, one of which is said to be of Aesculapius, the god of healing, who was born in what is now Cavtat. The main door leads to an atrium in which summer musical recitals are held. 🅐 Pred Dvorom 1 ❶ (020) 321 497 🕐 09.00–18.00 daily (summer); 09.00–16.00 daily (winter)

Orlando's Column

This doesn't look all that impressive, but when it was built in 1418 it was the focal point of the city-state, since government ordinances were promulgated here and punishments carried out. A flag with the 'Libertas' motto flies from the top and the start of the Dubrovnik Summer Festival (see page 14) is announced here. The medieval cult of Orlando (Roland) started in the 12th century and was based on the epic poem *Song of Roland*. 🅐 Luža Square

Palača Sponza (Sponza Palace)

Used as a customs house and mint, the Sponza Palace was built in the 16th century and grew rapidly as Dubrovnik's wealth multiplied. It is elaborately carved with Renaissance arches and Venetian Gothic windows, and currently houses the state archives. Exhibitions are often held inside the majestic courtyard and, during the Summer Festival, there are concerts. A room dedicated to the defenders

who lost their lives during the 1991 war (the Memorial Room of
the Defenders of Dubrovnik) is recommended for history buffs.
ⓐ Luža Square ⓒ 08.00–22.00 Mon–Sat, 10.00–22.00 Sun
(summer); 10.00–15.00 daily (winter)

Stradun (also known as Placa)

This is the city's main street, a pedestrian zone that runs from the
Pile to the Ploče gates along the line of a channel that once separated
the Roman settlement of Ragusa from the Slavic settlement of
Dubrovnik. Originally paved in the 15th century (and redone after
the earthquake in the 17th), the limestone pavement is polished
with centuries of use, so is shiny and extremely slippery when wet.

Velika Onofrijeva Fontana (Onofrio's Great Fountain)

Just inside the Pile Gate, this fountain (see map page 52), built in
1444, is shaped like a polygon and was once part of the city's water-
supply system. Topped by a bulbous dome, there are 14 masks
around the fountain that spout water. Visitors to the city were
required to wash here to guard against bringing in the plague. There
were once statues around the fountain as well, destroyed unfortunately
in the earthquake of 1667. Now the main human forms around it are
teenagers, who like to gather here to chat. ⓐ Near Pile Gate

Vrata od Pila (Pile Gate)

This entrance to the Old Town (see map page 52) dates back to 1471
and was approached across a wooden drawbridge that was pulled
up every night. Today it spans a dry moat with a garden. Just inside
the gate is the first glimpse you get of St Blaise, the city's patron
saint; nearby stands another statue, of famous Croatian sculptor
Ivan Meštrović.

WALKING TOURS

Dubrovnik is an ideal city for walking around, and an hour or two on the city walls is the best way to start. Within the old city, there's a good walk, starting outside the Pile Gate and ending at the Museum of Modern Art. The Pile Gate, which dates back to 1471, has a wooden drawbridge that used to be pulled up every night. Check out the statue of St Blaise and, further on, one by Ivan Meštrović. From here, head to the Stradun, once a marshy channel that separated the Roman settlement of Ragusa from Slavic Dubrovnik.

Just inside the Pile Gate, spend a bit of time photographing Onofrio's Great Fountain, built in 1444 as part of the city's plumbing system. The Franjevački Samostan (Franciscan Monastery) is next: take a good look at the exterior, but save the interior for a rainy day. At the far end of the Stradun, Orlando's Column in Luža Square symbolises the city's desire for freedom and marked the centre of town when it was built in 1418. On the left-hand side of the square, the Palača Sponza (Sponza Palace) holds the Memorial Room of the Defenders of Dubrovnik, the state archives and the original workings of the city clock. The clock tower with its astronomical clock is just behind Orlando's Column. Onofrio's Small Fountain, built in 1441, is next to the clock tower. From here, go along Sv Dominika to the Dominikanski Samostan (Dominican Monastery), out through the Ploče Gate to Frana Supila, and take a look at the first-class **Museum of Modern Art** (ⓐ Frana Supila 23 ⓣ (020) 426 590 ⓦ www.ugdubrovnik.hr ⓛ 10.00–20.00 Tues–Sun, closed Mon ⓘ Admission charge).

Rupe Ethnographic Museum

CULTURE

Kuća Marina Držića (Marin Držić House)

This is a theatrical museum, a scientific documentary institute and an exhibition space all rolled into one. It is named in memory of Marin Držić, one of Croatia's greatest playwrights. What makes this museum so unusual is that it's more of a theatrical experience than a museum: visitors find themselves surrounded by puppets, posters and typical stage props. Actors guide people through the exhibits in such a way that they feel like participants of a theatrical performance.
ⓐ Široka ulica 7 ❶ (020) 323 242 ❷ 10.00–17.00 Tues–Sun, closed Mon

Muzej Rupe (Rupe Ethnographic Museum)

This is a glimpse back to the 16th century: an immense stone barn with 15 huge storage pits that were used for keeping the municipal grain. At one time, these pits were dug into floors all over town, but this is the only one that has survived. The top floor houses an ethnographic exhibition of rural life and husbandry plus costumes, textiles and so on. ⓐ Ulica od Rupa 3 ❶ (020) 323 013 ❷ 09.00–16.00 Wed–Mon, closed Tues

Pomorski Muzej (Maritime Museum)

Located in St John's Fortress, the Maritime Museum (see map page 52) is of great interest to old salts and those interested in the background of this seafaring country. It looks at the history of Ragusan sea power, with model displays of boats throughout the centuries and marine artefacts. There are trade-route maps, sextants, and a particularly interesting, well-stocked 19th-century medicine chest, used by doctors on ships. ❶ (020) 323 904 ❷ 09.00–18.00 Tues–Sun, closed Mon in the summer, with shorter hours in the winter

Sinagoga i Židovski Muzej (Synagogue & Jewish Museum)
Dating from 1352, the second-oldest synagogue in Europe is set in the
former Jewish ghetto and is small but beautiful inside with its ornate
decorations and blue ceiling. The museum displays artefacts and tells
the history of Dubrovnik's age-old Jewish community. ② Žudioska 5
① (020) 321 028 ① 10.00–13.00 Mon–Fri (Feb, Mar & Dec);
10.00–15.00 Mon–Fri (Apr); 10.00–20.00 Mon–Fri (May–Nov);
closed Sat, Sun & Jan ① Admission charge

RETAIL THERAPY

The main artery for shopping is Stradun in the Old Town, where
you'll find clothing and shoe shops in the alleys that run off the
street. There's also a shop where the owner makes and sells candles.
If you are after items that 'say Dubrovnik', the embroidery distinctive
to the Konavle region south of the city is special. You can find napkins
and tablecloths at some of the better gift-shops, but they are pricey.
For traditional Croatian jewellery such as filigree earrings and coral
necklaces, try some of the jewellery shops at the western end of
Puča. Foreigners can claim a sales tax refund within one year for
anything they buy. Be sure to ask the salesperson to fill out the
tax-refund form when purchasing your goods.

There are two fruit and vegetable markets, one in the Old Town
on Gundulićeva poljana and the other one in Gruž. Both sell fresh
produce and are open every day until noon – or sometimes longer.

For opening hours, see page 147.

Alogoritam Books This is the best bookshop in town if you're
looking for books in English. They also have travel guides and maps.
② Placa 8 ① (020) 322 044

🔺 *Retail therapy is a must in Dubrovnik*

Arca Antique Shop A large selection of antique dishes, vases, glasses, tablecloths and paintings by Croatian artists. ⓐ Gundulićeva poljana

Art Studio 1 Hajdarhodžić Sells handmade clay ships and fishing boats, also some paintings and antiques. ⓐ Zlatarska 1

Dallas Croatian music CDs as well as international music. ⓐ Antuninska 2 ⓣ (020) 323 388

Euroshop A department store close to the market in Gruž. ⓐ Obala Ante Starčevića 25 ⓣ (020) 313 800 ⓦ www.euroshop.hr ⓝ Bus: line 3, 6 or 8 from Pile to Gruž

Franja Coffee & Teahouse Besides coffee and tea you can pick up great food gifts here. There's wild-rose brandy, herbal *rakija* wine made with the local grapes, figs in honey, olive oil and special liqueurs. ⓐ Od Puča 9 ⓣ (020) 324 816 ⓦ www.franja.hr

Kod Male Braće Pharmacy For a really unusual gift (and to treat yourself too), stop in at the still-functioning Franciscan Monastery pharmacy to check out the range of unusual lotions and creams, some formulated from recipes dating back to 1317. Some of the recommended ones are the lemon hand-lotion, rose or lavender face-cream, and the jojoba and menthol moisturiser. If you say it's a gift, they'll give you a special bag. ⓐ Placa 30 ⓣ (020) 321 411

Ronchi Hats This hat shop has been around since 1858 and has a rich array of, er, hats. ⓐ Lučarića 2, on a narrow lane near Market Square and Orlando monument ⓣ (020) 323 699 ⓦ www.dubrovnik-online.com/ronchi

TAKING A BREAK

Buffet Škola £ ❶ A family-run sandwich bar that makes delicious *pršut*-and-cheese sandwiches on home-made bread. ❸ Antuninska 1, a side street between Stradun and Prijeko ❶ (020) 321 096 ❶ 09.00–22.00 daily (summer); 09.00–21.00 daily (winter)

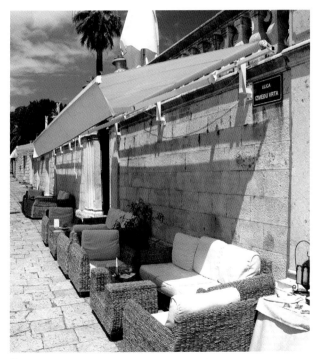

● *There are many comfy cafés dotted about the Old Town*

Buza £ ❷ Perched on the rocks just outside the Old Town's sea-facing walls, this waterfront bar has atmosphere. Look for the 'cold drinks' sign. Serves coffee, *travarica*, cool beer, lemonade and ice cream. ⓐ Ispod Mira ❶ (020) 324 053 ❻ 08.30–02.00 daily (summer); opening depends on weather (winter)

Festival £ ❸ A smart café with the best sticky cakes and Spanish hot chocolate in town. Excellent café breakfast as well. ⓐ Placa bb ❶ (020) 321 148 ❻ 07.00–24.00 daily

Gavun £ ❹ A venue that has fish and mussel sandwiches for a low-price lunch. ⓐ Široka ulica 3 ❶ (020) 323 205 ❻ 10.00–14.00, 18.00–21.00 daily

Gradska Kavana £ ❺ A cavernous café where locals come for cakes and ice cream on the terrace in warm weather or to listen to live piano in the summer. Lovely atmosphere. ⓐ Pred Dvorom 1 ❶ (020) 321 202 ❿ www.mea-culpa.hr ❻ 08.00–24.00 daily (summer); 08.00–23.00 daily (winter)

AFTER DARK

You'll be spoilt for choice in terms of restaurants, with the busiest ones being in the Old Town along a street called Prijeko and off Široka ulica. Some of these are closed in the winter. Menus tend to be similar, with heavy emphasis on seafood, grilled meat, pizza and other Croatian specialities like *rižot* (seafood risotto), *meneštra* (minestrone soup) and *buzara* (langoustines in a tomato sauce). Many of the more popular restaurants require a reservation and make a small cover charge.

RESTAURANTS

Kamenica £ ❻ A no-frills eatery with seafood and fresh oysters.
ⓐ Gundulićeva poljana 8, near the open-air market ❶ (020) 323 682
🕒 08.00–23.30 daily (summer); 08.00–16.00 daily (winter)

Mea Culpa £ ❼ Good pizza cooked in a wood-fired oven and other
Italian dishes. There are tables on the street and draught Guinness®.
ⓐ Za Rokom 3 ❶ (020) 323 430 Ⓦ www.mea-culpa.hr 🕒 08.00–
01.00 daily (summer); 08.00–23.00 daily (winter); closed Jan

Spaghetteria Toni £ ❽ Come here for strong Turkish coffee and
what the locals claim is the best pasta (especially the lasagna) in
town. Good soups and bruschettas too. ⓐ Nikole Božidarevića 14
❶ (020) 323 134 🕒 10.00–24.00 daily (summer); closed winter

Marco Polo ££ ❾ Tiny restaurant, but in the summer you can dine
in the courtyard on typical dishes such as *crni rižot* (black risotto
in cuttlefish ink). ⓐ Lučarica 6, on a side street behind the Crkva Sv
Vlaha (Church of St Blaise) ❶ (020) 323 719 🕒 10.00–24.00 daily

Orsan Gverović ££ ❿ On the sea in Zaton Mali, 7 km (4^1/$_3$ miles)
west of Dubrovnik, stands this seafood restaurant. It is housed in a
genuine, ancient *orsan* (boat house). ⓐ Štikovica 43 ❶ (020) 891 267
Ⓦ www.gverovic-orsan.hr 🕒 12.00–24.00 daily (summer); closed
winter 🚍 Bus: line 12 or 15 from Gruž

Atlas Club Nautika £££ ⓫ Considered to be the best place in town for
quality seafood, with grand dining rooms, an outdoor terrace, formal
waiters, and an international wine list. ⓐ Brsalje 3 Ⓦ www.esculap-
teo.hr ❶ (020) 442 526 🕒 12.00–24.00 daily (summer); closed winter

Gil's £££ 🅓 Excellent French food in an elegant restaurant inside St Luke's bastion. The Pop Lounge, on the upper level with sea views, is great for cocktails. ⓐ Sv Dominika bb ⓣ (020) 322 222 ⓦ www. gilsdubrovnik.com ⓛ 12.00–02.00 daily (summer); closed winter

Proto £££ 🅔 Proto has been around since 1886 and is known for its fish specialities prepared from old recipes of Dubrovnik fishermen. Formal dining room with relaxed outdoor terrace and meticulous service. Excellent local wine list. ⓐ Široka ulica 1 ⓣ (020) 323 234 ⓛ 11.00–24.00 daily (summer); 11.00–23.00 daily (winter)

BARS, CLUBS & DISCOS

Belvedere East of the Old Town, amazing parties are held on the terraces of this abandoned hotel, with revellers dancing until well after sunrise. It has a private beach too. ⓐ Hotel Belvedere, Župa Dubrovačka ⓛ 08.00–04.00 Fri & Sat (summer); closed winter

Capitano Swings on Friday nights, with a young crowd. ⓐ Između vrta 2, near Pile Gate ⓣ (098) 366 470 ⓛ 20.00–04.00 daily (summer); 20.00–04.00 Thur–Sat, closed Sun–Wed (winter)

Katie O'Connor's Irish Pub Lively all year round, this cellar pub has everything you need to feel at home: sports on TV, pub grub on your plate and free Wi-Fi for your phone. ⓐ Dropčeva 4A ⓣ (020) 321 575 ⓦ www.katieoconnors.com ⓛ 10.00–02.00 daily

Latino Club Fuego Probably the most popular club in Dubrovnik, with good music and reasonable prices. ⓐ Brsalje 8, near Pile Gate ⓣ (020) 312 870 ⓦ www.dubrovniknightclub.com ⓛ 23.00–06.00 daily (summer); 23.00–06.00 Fri & Sat, closed Sun–Thur (winter)

Lazareti A club with everything from theatre and dance to alternative music. ⓐ Frana Supila 8 ⓣ (020) 324 633 ⓦ www.arl.hr ⓛ 21.00–04.00 daily (summer); special events/parties only (winter)

Libertina Tiny place and a good spot to meet local people. ⓐ Zlatarska 3, a side street next to Sponza Palace ⓣ (020) 321 526 ⓛ 10.00–14.00, 19.00–21.00 daily

Nonenina A small Old Town café; at night a great place for cocktails and local wines. ⓐ Pred Dvorom 4 ⓣ (098) 915 9909 ⓦ www. nonenina.com ⓛ 09.00–02.00 daily

Orlandinjo Club Upmarket club with excellent jazz and other live acts. ⓐ Hotel Dubrovnik Palace, Masarykov put 20 ⓣ (020) 430 000 ⓛ 22.00–04.00 Tues–Sat, closed Sun & Mon

Sesame Bar Live music at weekends. Very intimate interior, but outdoor seating too. ⓐ Dante Alighieria bb, five minutes west of Pile Gate ⓣ (020) 412 910 ⓦ www.sesame.hr ⓛ 08.00–23.00 daily (summer); 12.00–16.00, 18.00–22.00 Mon–Sat, closed Sun (winter)

SkyBar One of the most modern venues in town, you can have Wi-Fi with your breakfast here, a bite of lunch or dinner, or join the trendy crowds at night for their great cocktails. ⓐ Marojice Kaboge 1 ⓣ (091) 220 2094 ⓛ 09.00–02.00 daily

Talir If you are here for the Summer Festival (see page 14), this is the place to meet actors and musicians. ⓐ Antuninska bb ⓛ 08.00–02.00 Fri & Sat, 08.00–24.00 Sun–Thur (summer); 08.00–24.00 daily (winter)

Korčula

This is the sixth-largest Adriatic island – and one of the greenest – with a good smattering of vineyards and olive groves. Because of the mild climate, there's a variety of vegetation, from conifer forests and meadows of wild flowers to a typically Mediterranean coastline with coves and beaches. The walled town of Korčula, with all its historic associations, is why people mainly come to the island, but it's also interesting as a slice of traditional life. The population here is quite devout and the people observe many ancient religious ceremonies as well as keeping alive folk dances, songs, music and traditional costumes.

Korčula was first settled by the Greeks, but it wasn't until it was ruled by Venice that it became prosperous because of its flourishing shipbuilding industry. Stone was also quarried on the island by skilled local artisans and cut for export. Korčula's growth and expansion was brought to an end after a catastrophic outbreak of the plague in 1529, and the decline continued as Mediterranean trade diminished following the discovery of America. It wasn't until the early 20th century and the development of tourism that Korčula began to emerge from obscurity.

The main ferry to Dubrovnik from Rijeka in northern Croatia stops at the harbour of Korčula Town, along with other daily ferries making the run from Split to Vela Luka. By bus, there's a daily service from Dubrovnik that crosses the narrow stretch of water between the mainland and the island on a car ferry from Orebić. The bus station is 200 m (219 yds) southeast of the Old Town. The tourist information office (ⓐ Obala dr Franje Tuđmana 4 ⓣ (020) 715 701 ⓦ www.visitkorcula.net) is on the western side of the town.

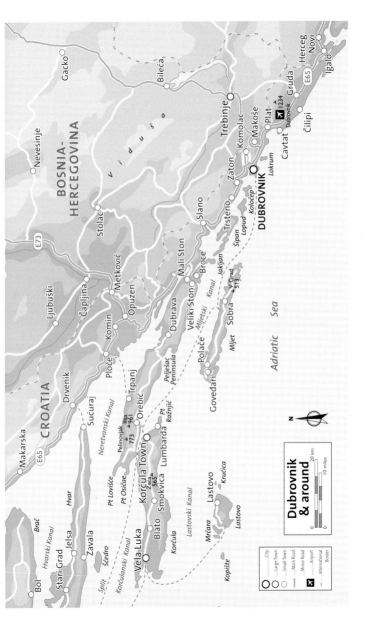

CROATIA

BOSNIA-
HERCEGOVINA

Vidusa

Adriatic Sea

Makarska

Brač

Hvarski Kanal

Hvar

Bol

Stari Grad

Jelsa

Zavala

Šćedro

Split

Korčulanski Kanal

Vela Luka

Blato

Korčula

Smokvica

Lumbarda

Korčula Town

Zrnovo 565

Kopište

Mrčara

Lastovo

Kručica

Lastovo

Lastovski Kanal

Lastovo

Sućuraj

Drvenik

E65

Ploče

Tirpanj

Orebić

Pt Osičac

Pt Lovišće

Pelinovjak 773

Ilija 961

Neretvanski Kanal

Pt Ražnjić

Komin

Opuzen

Metković

Čapljina

Ljubuški

E73

Stolac

Nevesinje

Gacko

Bileća

Trebinje

Dubrava

Veliki Ston

Mali Ston

Broce

Pelješac Peninsula

Polače

Govedari

Mljet

Sobra

Mljetski Kanal

Jakljan

Grad 513

Slano

Trsteno

Zaton

Komolac

Makoše

Plat

Dubrovnik 1234

Cavtat

Čilipi

Gruda

Herceg Novi

Igalo

E65

Šipan

Lopud

Koločep

Lokrum

DUBROVNIK

N

Dubrovnik & around

0   20 km
0   10 miles

City
Large Town
Small Town
Main Road
Minor Road
Airport
International
Border

SIGHTS & ATTRACTIONS

From a bird's point-of-view, Korčula Town, the island's main settlement, looks like a fish on a platter with a central spine and ribs branching off on each side. This layout dates back to the 13th century, and was meant to reduce the effects of wind and sun. The town rises above its 13th-century walls like a mini-Dubrovnik. There is a distinct Venetian flavour to the architecture and culture – little wonder, because the Venetians took control of the island in the 10th century and stayed on for more than eight centuries. Most of the buildings date to the town's Golden Age (13th–15th centuries), including one remaining town wall in the south; most of the others were demolished in the 19th century. The town has a special beauty, with its elegant 19th-century staircase sweeping up to Kopnena Vrata (Land Gate), the main entrance to the Old Town. This gate was completed in the 15th century along with the Revelin, the hulk of a defensive tower looming above it.

Beaches

While there are beaches in town, they're usually crowded and rocky, so the best bet is to take the bus to Lumbarda, about 8 km (5 miles) south of Korčula Town – the beaches are a 20-minute walk from the bus station but the great sand on Prižna Bay is worth it. Bilin Žal, just a short distance away, is rockier but has great views of the coastal mountains.

Katedrala Sv Marka (St Mark's Cathedral)

This magnificent 15th-century limestone structure dominates Cathedral Square; it was built in the Gothic-Renaissance style by local and Italian workmen. It has an interesting portal decorated

Korčula Town

0 — 25 metres
0 — 25 yards

N

Korčulanski Kanal

St Barbara's Tower

Bokar Tower

Tourist boats to Orebić

Orebić

POI
Cathedral
Information
Bus Station

SPANIĆEVA

ANTINA ROŽANOVIĆA

ROŽANOVIĆA

SV ROKA

BISK. LUKE TOLENTIĆA

KORČUL BRATOŠTINA

POMENICA

ŠETALIŠTE PETRA KANAVELIĆA

IVANA VIDALIJA

Kuća Marco Polo

DEPOLO

DR VINKA FORETIĆA

DON PAVLA

RAFA ARNERIJA

Gradski Muzej

Katedrala Sv Marka

KALAFATA

Morska Vrata

DR DINKA MIROŠEVIĆA

TRG SV MARKA

BISKUPIJE

ISMAELLI

Church of Our Lady

MARKA ANDRIJIĆA

GIUNIO

KORČULANSKOG STATUTA

BANIĆEVIĆA

OD TEATRA

LJUBE BABIĆA

Galerija Ikona

ŽITNICA

KAPOROVA

Crkva Sv Mihovila

All Saints' Church

KNEŽEV PROLAZ

TRG KORČULANSKIH KLESARA I KIPARA

Kopnena Vrata

FOŠA

Revelin Tower

DOBROTVORNOSTI

RAMPADA

OBALA HRVATSKIH MORNARA

Market

Badija Island

PLOKATA 19 TRAVNJA

Jadrolinija

Campsite & Park Hotel (Bike hire),
Car ferry to Orebić &
Lumbarda Beach

OBALA VINKA PALETINA

with a two-tailed mermaid, an elephant and other sculptures. On the façade, there's a beautiful fluted rose window and a strange cornice filled with even stranger beasts. Inside, look for the modern *Pičta* by famous sculptor Ivan Meštrović, and an altarpiece painting by Tintoretto. There's also a bronze statue of St Blaise by Meštrović.

Kuća Marco Polo (Marco Polo's House)

This is a 17th-century house that allegedly marks the spot where Marco Polo, adventurer, merchant and author of the world's first travel book, was born (see below). You can climb up to the tower-like upper storeys for a great view of the terracotta rooftops of the town.

MARCO POLO LIVED HERE, PERHAPS

Despite a shortage of hard evidence, Korčulans insist that their island was the birthplace of the famous explorer. One firm bit of documentation says that Marco Polo was captured by the Genoese in a sea battle off Korčula in 1298; perhaps he was visiting relatives (there is a family on the island named de Polo). Korčulans insist, in any event, that Polo was born in 1254, went to Venice with his family in 1269, travelled the world and then, after being captured by the Genoese, was tossed into jail. It was during this period in jail that he wrote his famous book of adventures. What is certain is that he led an action-packed life, spending 17 years in China as a close personal friend of Kublai Khan. His famous travelogue sparked much interest in the Far East. Wherever he was born, the Korčulans are his biggest fans, and make a point of throwing celebrations to mark the key events in his life.

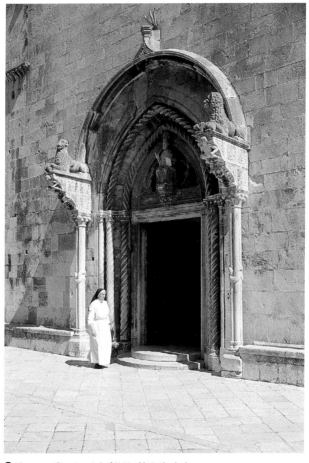

⬥ *The magnificent portal of St Mark's Cathedral*

◔ *Green hills and blue seas frame the picturesque town of Korčula*

📍 In the alley Depolo 🌐 www.czk-korcula.com 🕐 10.00–14.00 daily (mid-Apr–May, Sept & Oct); 09.00–21.00 daily (June–Aug); closed Nov–mid-April

Town walls & towers

The whole town is surrounded by robust 13th- to 15th-century walls and towers: there were a total of 12 in the Middle Ages. There are two principal entrances: Kopnena Vrata (Land Gate) and the Morska Vrata (Sea Gate) on the west. The Revelin Tower, built by the Venetians in the 15th century, is topped with a terrace from which there are excellent views.

CULTURE

Galerija Ikona (Museum of Icons)

A permanent display of icons held by the All Saints' Brotherhood, including a haunting 15th-century triptych of the Passion and Byzantine icons painted on wood, as well as some 17th- and 18th-century ritual objects. 📍 Trg Sv Svetih, near Kaporova 📞 (020) 711 306 🕐 10.00–12.00, 17.00–19.00 (July & Aug); closed Sept–June

Gradski Muzej (Town Museum)

Housed in a Venetian palace located on the main square, the town museum stands just opposite the cathedral. The collection here includes historical items related to Korčula's history, including a copy of a 4th-century BC Greek tablet from Lumbarda, plus a room upstairs done up to show a typical Korčulan peasant kitchen. 📍 Trg Sv Marka 📞 (020) 711 420 🌐 www.gm-korcula.com 🕐 10.00–14.00, 18.00–20.00 Mon–Sat, closed Sun (summer); 10.00–14.00 Mon–Fri, closed Sat & Sun (winter)

RETAIL THERAPY

The main things to take home from Korčula and the Pelješac
Peninsula are wine and foodstuffs, particularly the produce of the
local vineyards and olive groves. Dingač is the area's most famous
red wine and is hard to find outside Croatia. Its slightly sweet
flavour is reckoned to emanate from the grapes being partially dried
before being crushed. It certainly benefits greatly from the area's
sun-drenched limestone soils. The best plan is to go directly to the
producer at wineries on the island. Olive oils are produced all
through the country, but buying directly from the Korčulan grower
seems to add a special quality to the oil.

TAKING A BREAK

Cukarin £ ❶ A sweet shop famous for its selection of home-baked
biscuits and other delicious goodies. ⓐ Ulica Hrvatske bratske
zajednice bb, near Plokata 19 travnja ⓣ (020) 711 055 ⓦ www.
cukarin.hr ⓛ 08.30–12.30, 17.30–20.30 Mon–Fri (Easter–Oct);
closed Sat, Sun & Nov–Mar

Kiwi £ ❷ A good bet for a cool, soothing ice cream. ⓐ Biline 16, near
Plokata 19 travnja ⓣ (020) 715 781 ⓛ 08.00–24.00 Mon–Sat, closed
Sun (summer); 08.00–15.00 Mon–Sat, closed Sun (winter)

Grubinjac ££ ❸ An old rustic farmhouse on the way from Korčula
to Žrnovo village, with great views over the hills beyond. Meals
and snacks can be served on the terrace with the restaurant's
home-produced wine. ⓐ Grubinjac bb, near Plokata 19 travnja
ⓣ (020) 711 410 ⓛ 18.00–24.00 daily (May–Oct); closed Nov–Apr

AFTER DARK

RESTAURANTS

Zalogajnica Maslina £ ❹ Wonderful, fresh local food served in a lovely family-run restaurant just south of town. ⓐ Lumbarajska cesta ❶ (020) 711 720 ⏱ 12.00–23.00 daily

Konoba Marinero ££ ❺ Offers home-made specialities and delicious grilled fish in a room filled with maritime bric-a-brac, or out on the terrace squeezed into a narrow alley. ⓐ Ulica Marka Andrijića 13 (just off Pjace main square) ❶ (020) 711 170 ⏱ 12.00–23.00 daily (May–Oct); closed Nov–Apr

Morski Konjić ££ ❻ A cosy little restaurant at the northern tip of town between St Barbara's and Bokar towers; it is hung with fishing nets and serves a selection of meats and fish. ⓐ Šetalište Petra Kanavelića 1 ❶ (020) 711 642 ⏱ 12.00–24.00 daily

Planjak ££ ❼ An established and unpretentious place with a full range of grilled food, especially grilled kebabs. The restaurant has a shaded terrace. ⓐ Plokata 19 travnja 19 ❶ (020) 711 015 ⏱ 08.00–24.00 Mon–Sat, closed Sun (summer); 08.00–15.00 Mon–Sat, closed Sun (winter)

Kanavelić ££–£££ ❽ Kanavelić specialises in very fresh fish and seafood including mussels washed down with the best local wines. Try the octopus salad. This is considered formal dining – the grilled scampi are a speciality. ⓐ Sv Barbara 12, near Hotel Korčula ❶ (020) 711 800 ⏱ 12.00–23.00 daily (May–Oct); closed Nov–Apr

BARS & CLUBS

Nightlife in Korčula is limited to a couple of bars and the island's hotels, where live performers entertain guests.

Cocktail Bar Massimo A quirky bar on top of one of the Zakerjan towers in the city wall on the northern tip of the Old Town. Visitors ascend an extremely steep staircase; drinks are hoisted up in a special lift. ⓐ Šetalište Petra Kanavelića bb ⓘ 12.00–24.00 daily

Dos Locos A bar with lots of outdoor seating and a lively atmosphere. ⓐ Šetalište Franje Kršinića 14, south of the Old Town

ACCOMMODATION

HOTELS & GUESTHOUSES

Bon Repos ££ On the road to Lumbarda, this is a large hotel complex with pool and comfortable rooms. ⓐ Dubrovačka cesta 19 ⓘ (020) 726 880 ⓦ www.korcula-hotels.com

Korčula ££ This is the oldest of the town's hotels and was the town hall during Austrian times. The rooms are comfy, if slightly frayed. ⓐ Obala dr Franje Tuđmana 5 ⓘ (020) 726 480 ⓦ www.korcula-hotels.com

Park ££ This hotel won't win any architectural awards, but there is a beach and many of the rooms have balconies. ⓐ Šetalište Franje Kršinića 102 ⓘ (020) 726 336 ⓦ www.korcula-hotels.com

Lešić Dimitri Palace £££ Six stunning 'residencies' in an 18th-century bishop's palace and several adjoining houses in Korčula's Old Town.

The apartments have stylish décor and sea views, and the hotel has several boats for guests to use. ⓐ Don Pavla 1–6 ⓣ (020) 715 560 ⓦ www.lesic-dimitri.com ⓛ Apr–Oct

APARTMENTS

With hotel accommodation distinctly limited in Korčula Town, there are at least a number of private rooms and apartments available. It's best to deal with one of the agencies in town that do the booking for these, such as **Korčula Travel** (ⓐ Trg Sv Justine 8 ⓣ (020) 612 058 ⓦ www.korcula-travel.com) or **Kantun Tours** (ⓐ Plokata bb ⓣ (020) 715 622 ⓦ www.kantun-tours.com). Both operate from April to October.

⬥ The narrow streets of Korčula Town

Cavtat

Sitting on a peninsula between two bays, Cavtat (pronounced 'Tsavtat') lies about 16 km (10 miles) south of Dubrovnik and makes a good day trip or short visit. Even though Cavtat is popular with packaged tours, the hotel area is away from the village centre so the place still exudes a bit of charm. The seafront promenade is lined with bars, restaurants and palm trees, giving it a Mediterranean feel, and about 1 km ($^2/_3$ mile) east of the town centre there's a *žal* or beach area.

Originally a colony founded by Greeks and known as Epidaurum, Cavtat went through the usual period of invasion and pillaging before establishing itself as a fishing village. It was rediscovered in the early 20th century and became the playground of the rich.

Bus No 10 runs to Cavtat from Dubrovnik every hour, and there are a couple of ferry companies, with varying timetables, that serve the route. For people visiting Croatia by car, Cavtat is a good alternative to staying in Dubrovnik: the accommodation tends to be more reasonably priced and there are no parking problems.

SIGHTS & ATTRACTIONS

The town's best beaches lie to the east and west, about 1 km ($^2/_3$ mile) to the east where all the large package hotels are, and to the west in front of the hotel Croatia (see page 91). There are also pleasant walks around the headlands where you can swim off the rocks.

Funerary sights may not be on everyone's 'must-do' list but there is one that should be seen. Sitting on a beautiful hilltop overlooking the sea, the showpiece is the **Račić Mausoleum**, built by famous sculptor Ivan Meštrović for the daughter of a wealthy ship-owning family (it was rumoured that Meštrović was her lover). This white marble sepulchre was built in 1922 and is an eclectic mix of angels, eagles, dogs and so on. After the monument was completed, the entire family died in quick succession.

AFTER DARK

RESTAURANTS

Konoba Kolona £ A budget restaurant serving tasty fare. Shady terrace near the bus stop. ⓐ Put Od Tihe 2 ⓣ (020) 478 787 ⓒ 12.00–23.00 daily (May–Oct); closed Nov–Apr

THE TALENTED MR BUKOVAC

Formerly the home of Vlaho Bukovac, a talented painter born in Cavtat, **Galerija Bukovac** (ⓐ Ulica Vlahe Bukovca 5 ⓣ (020) 478 646 ⓦ www.kuca-bukovac.hr) is now a gallery dedicated to his works. Bukovac studied in Paris and travelled widely through Europe before returning to Croatia and playing an important role in the development of Croatian art. His paintings – portraits as well as many other subjects – combine a photographic realism with touches of Impressionism. Bukovac ended his career as a professor of fine arts in Prague.

In the centre of town, the 16th-century **Knežev Dvor** (Rector's Palace, ⓣ (020) 478 556) holds more of Vlaho Bukovac's work, along with drawings by Croatian and foreign artists, old coins, and a lapidarium with Roman stone pieces from the 1st century AD. It is also known as the Baltazar Bogisic Collection, after a lawyer and cultural activist who spent his life promoting Croatian literature and learning.

○ *Deliciously fresh fish is served everywhere in the region*

Feral Restaurant ££ Good food and entertainment each weekend.
ⓐ Obala Ante Starčevića 66 ⓣ (020) 478 034

Konavoski Dvori ££–£££ For a grand meal out, this is a highly praised
restaurant beside a working watermill on the River Ljuta about 18 km
(11 miles) east of Cavtat. Waitresses wear the local Konavoski
costume and specialities of the house include lamb and trout.
ⓐ Pridvorje Ljuta, Konavle ⓣ (020) 791 039 ⓦ www.esculap-teo.hr
ⓛ 12.00–24.00 daily (Apr–Nov); closed Dec–Mar

Leut ££–£££ Conveniently located in the centre of town, this
restaurant has been around for three decades serving fresh and
delicious seafood. A comfortable outdoor terrace is open in the
summer months. ⓐ Trumbićev put 11 ⓣ (020) 478 477 ⓛ 11.00–24.00
daily (Mar–Nov); closed Dec–Feb

ACCOMMODATION

Supetar £ Right in the centre of town, on the harbourfront, this is
an older hotel that has been tastefully modernised. ⓐ Obala Ante
Starčevića 27 ⓣ (020) 475 777 ⓦ www.hotelsupetar.com

Albatros ££ This is one of the beachfront hotels that caters for package
holiday guests. It has a private swimming pool and rooms have air
conditioning. ⓐ Od Žala 1 ⓣ (020) 481 550 ⓦ www.iberostar.com

Croatia ££ This is a huge, 487-room, 5-star hotel on the ridge of the
Sustjepan Peninsula. It offers all the amenities: TV, air conditioning,
swimming pool and private beaches, nudist and otherwise. ⓣ (020)
475 555 ⓦ www.hotelcroatia.hr

The Elaphite Islands

This string of 'car-less' islands, 14 in all (three of which are inhabited), lies between Dubrovnik and the Pelješac Peninsula. They are considered one of Croatia's 'best-kept secrets'. What they offer is an area of rich vegetation, unspoilt nature (their name means 'Deer') and a long architectural heritage. Dotted here and there are 15th- and 16th-century Gothic and Renaissance churches together with some pre-Romanesque chapels. Dubrovnik, with its shifting cultures, casts a strong influence over the Elaphites and their villages.

Ferries leave several times a day from Dubrovnik for the main Elaphite Islands. Once there, visitors get around on foot, since cars are not allowed. For Lokrum there are boats leaving on the half-hour every day during high season and on weekends from the port in Dubrovnik's Old Town. Out of season, there are people with private boats who may take you across. Ask around.

SIGHTS & ATTRACTIONS

Koločep

Less than a half-hour away by ferry, this is the first of the inhabited Elaphite Isles and a very easy day trip. There are two small villages, Donje Čelo and Gornje Čelo, on an island that is just over 2.5 sq km (1 sq mile) in area and that has a population of around 150 people.

The recommendation here is to walk through the sweet-smelling pine and deciduous forests, with perhaps a picnic halfway through. In season (after May) you can end the day eating freshly grilled seafood at a couple of restaurants on the waterfront. The only accommodation is the **Villas Koločep** (● (020) 757 025 ● www. kolocep.com), a group of eight modern units above Donje Čelo beach.

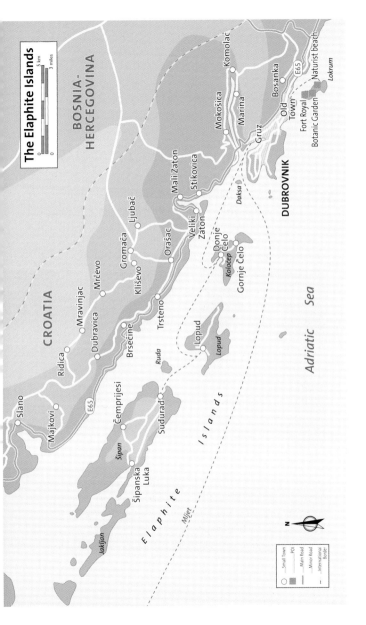

Lopud

Just beyond Koločep, Lopud was once a lively retreat for the noble families of Dubrovnik and remnants of their palatial houses can still be found. On the northern end of the island, the village of Lopud curves around a wide bay and a sandy beach.

Šipan

Šipan, aka 'The Golden Island', is the largest of the Elaphites, and yet the least developed. The main attractions here are the peace, quiet

● *Lopud was once a favoured retreat for noble families*

and gentle walks, especially the 7-km (4¹/₃-mile) walk or bike ride
from Suđurađ to Šipanska Luka on the island's northern end, which
passes groves of figs, grapes and olives. There's a small sandy beach
here and some good isolated spots for sunbathing, as well as a fine
ruined villa on the harbourfront.

CULTURE

The main relic of Lopud's more vigorous past life is a fortified
Franciscan monastery and **Crkva Gospe od Špilice** (Church of Our
Lady of the Rocks) with its collection of altar paintings. The small

LOKRUM – PARADISE, CROATIAN STYLE

Lokrum is a tiny island, just 2 km (1¼ miles) long. According to local legend, one of its earliest famous visitors came a trifle unwillingly. Richard the Lionheart, on his way home from the Crusades in 1192, encountered a fierce storm offshore. Like others facing shipwreck, he vowed that – if he was saved – he would build a church in thanks. He landed on Lokrum to fulfil his promise, but was persuaded that his money would be better spent if he built in Ragusa (Dubrovnik) rather than on an insignificant island.

Just 15 minutes by boat from the quay in Dubrovnik's Old Town, subtropical, uninhabited Lokrum is wonderfully undeveloped. Peace and tranquillity reign, and the biggest attractions are the beaches (cleaner and less crowded than Dubrovnik) and a network of trails that criss-crosses the island. Lokrum also has a protected **naturist beach**, one of the country's premier nudist beaches, on the southeastern end, and a warm, saltwater lake. The island has a great variety of flora including an old **Botanic Garden** with palms, cacti, vines, Australian eucalyptus, ancient trees and herbs running rampant. The garden was established in 1959 as an experiment to see if tropical plants would grow from seed and thrive in a Mediterranean climate.

Fort Royal is a fortress in the Lokrum hills, built in the shape of a star by the French in 1806. It's a steep, 20-minute hike up rickety steps, but from the top there are great views of Dubrovnik, Cavtat and the islands.

museum and treasury at the end of the harbour has a series of
9th- to 11th-century frescoes in bad condition, some icons and
other sacred objects and an assortment of other historic bits and
pieces, from 500-year-old pudding bowls to 200-year-old French
bayonets. Steps lead up to a ruined palace and private chapel built
for Miho Pracat, a somewhat legendary 16th-century shipowner
and merchant who allegedly saved Spain from starvation and made
himself a fortune at the same time. His bust stands in the Knežev
Dvor (Rector's Palace) in Dubrovnik (see page 63).

In Šipan, ruined villas are scattered all over the island,
remnants of an era when Dubrovnik was powerful, along with
ruined churches going back many centuries. In Suđurađ, the ferry's
first stop, there are the ruins of a summer palace built by a 16th-
century shipowner.

ACCOMMODATION

There are no hotels or restaurants on Lokrum. In Lopud, the tourist
office (🄰 Obala Iva Kuljevana 12 🄣 (020) 759 086 🄛 May–mid-Oct)
has a list of rooms for anyone wishing to stay longer than a day;
rooms can also be viewed and booked via 🅦 www.lopud.eu. There
are two hotels, the **Lafodia** (🄰 Obala Iva Kuljevana 51 🄣 (020) 759
022 🅦 www.lafodia.hr) and **Villa Vilina** (🄰 Obala Iva Kuljevana 5
🄣 (020) 759 333 🅦 www.villa-vilina.hr). Private rooms are available
on Šipan Island for overnighters and there is a harbourside hotel,
the **Šipan** (🄰 Šipanska luka 160 🄣 (020) 754 900 🅦 www.hotel-
sipan.hr). You will find a couple of bars and the hotel has a
restaurant, but there is absolutely no nightlife on the island.

Mljet

Mljet, perhaps Dalmatia's most beautiful island, with its steep rocky cliffs, has remained almost untouched through the centuries and has a mystery or two. Even though Malta lays claim to the legend of Calypso and Ulysses and the visit of St Paul after a shipwreck, Mljet may be a more likely base for the stories. Once called Melita, it was infested with snakes until the 19th century and St Paul was supposedly bitten by one (Malta has no snakes). The mongoose was imported to Mljet to control the snake. The mongooses flourished and multiplied, thereby curing the snake problem but causing a mongoose problem in the process. The island's vast National Park (see page 100), which occupies the entire western end of the island, is what mainly draws visitors to Mljet. It can be done in a day trip. A single road runs the length of the island.

The crossing from Dubrovnik takes four hours on the daily Jadrolinija ferry and in the summer one-and-a-half hours on the fast Jadrolinija or G&V catamarans that leave Dubrovnik in the morning and return in the afternoon. The ferries dock just to the east of Sobra and there are buses that take you into town, but there can be a problem in the summer when there are more passengers than buses. For day-trippers, catamarans dock at Polače. To get away from transportation headaches, the best idea is to book an all-inclusive package deal from one of the travel agencies; these include ferry, a tour, a chance to swim and a trip out to the island on the lake.

Aside from the buses that meet the ferries, there's no local transport. However, you can hire bikes, cars or scooters from several outlets, the biggest of which is the Hotel Odisej (see page 102) in Pomena. For more information on Mljet, contact the tourist office in Sobra (❶ (020) 746 025 ❿ www.mljet.hr).

SIGHTS & ATTRACTIONS

Mljet National Park

This is a Croatian national treasure and, besides the peace and tranquillity, the lack of commercial development is the main attraction of the island.

Since it was never ruled by Venice, no trees were chopped down to build major towns, and so the pine and oak forest with its two saltwater lakes has remained unspoilt. The larger of these two lakes, Veliko Jezero (Big Lake), has an island, Sv Marije, with a charming – but rundown – 12th-century monastery and church, **Crkva Sv Marije**, where you can still see parts of Romanesque and Renaissance architecture. Underneath lie Roman remains and there are foundations of other Roman buildings on the island.

The monastery was a hotel in its last incarnation but, since being returned to the Benedictines, restoration has begun and there are Sunday services in the church. You can visit the monastery gardens when they are open and there is a restaurant on the island where lunch is served (❶ (020) 744 145 Ⓦ www.mljet-restoranmelita.com).

The island also has a ten-minute walk where you can gather wild asparagus in the summer or visit two simple chapels built by sailors. A network of paths criss-crosses the park for walking or mountain biking, and there's a 9-km (5¹/₂-mile) trail that runs around the perimeter of the lakes. For a great view of the Pelješac Peninsula and the island of Korčula, there's a steep path up to the highest point in the park, Montokuc. There are boats in Pristanište that shuttle visitors back and forth to the island several times a day, with the fee included in the national park entry. Ⓦ www.mljet.hr Ⓦ www.zakladasvetemarije.hr

◐ The island of Mljet is beautiful and unspoilt

Odisejeva spilja (Ulysses' Cave)

According to legend, Ulysses stayed here for seven years during his epic voyage. Whether this is true or not, there is a cave directly south of Babino Polje that can be explored by boat (the easier way) or by trekking across the fields for a half-hour or so and climbing down to the cave.

Polače

The main attraction of this harbour town are the remains of a Roman palace with fortifications that lie just above the town, and the ruins of an ancient Christian basilica in a sheltered bay.

Saplunara

This stunning sand beach below Saplunara village is a great day trip or two- or three-day getaway. Families let rooms during the season and there are a couple of basic fish restaurants — and for total relaxation, you can get rid of clothes at a long, deserted, sandy nudist beach that is a 20-minute walk from Saplunara.

TAKING A BREAK

In Pomena, a favourite docking site for yachtsmen, there is a string of small restaurants along the harbour and in Polače there are a couple of small restaurants, a provisions store that is open in the mornings and a bakery. The restaurant at the monastery also serves good lunches.

ACCOMMODATION

Private rooms and campsites that are clean and comfortable are available in Pomena and Polače at reasonable prices, but

A DIVER'S PARADISE

Jacques Cousteau praised the Adriatic coast as one of the world's greatest dive locations and for good reason: the coastal waters are crystal clear and hold some very good dive attractions. One of these is an ancient Roman vessel where little remains but some amphorae; a more modern location is a German U-boat. Divers must pay an initial fee of 100kn at one of the registered dive centres or at the local harbourmaster's office before they can dive. For novices, there is an increasing number of dive shops opening up all along the Adriatic coast, offering lessons, equipment rental and guided trips. Around Mljet, diving is restricted to organised groups. For more information on diving, contact the **Croatian Diving Federation** (⊜ Dalmatinska 12, Zagreb Ⓦ www.diving.hr).

these should be booked in advance. The tourist office in Sobra (① (020) 746 025) can supply the names of people who will rent rooms. For booking ahead, try **Mini Brum** tourist agency (① (020) 745 084) in Babino Polje. There are also campsites in Babino Polje and in Ropa and a few run by private individuals. Ask a local for more information.

Odisej £££ In Pomena there is a modern 3-star hotel that is open from Easter until November. It has 155 rooms, some with a balcony and sea view, plus 2 luxury apartments. The hotel lies in the national park and is a 15-minute walk from Malo Jezero, so it makes a good base for a hiking holiday. ⊜ Pomena bb ① (020) 362 111 Ⓦ www.hotelodisej.hr ⏱ Easter–Nov

Pelješac Peninsula

This is one of those places that people can often pass straight through without knowing what they're missing. Geographically (see map page 77), it's a long, narrow peninsula – 62 km (39 miles) long but never more than 7 km (4^1/$_3$ miles) wide. It feels like an island, though, and there's the sense of always being near water. Isolated and undeveloped, Pelješac is mainly known for its two excellent wines (Postup and Dingač), both of which can be tasted in cellars that are open to the public in the summer. Ragusa (Dubrovnik) owned the peninsula from the 12th to the early 19th century, and many of the republic's finest seafarers came from this region.

Buses from Dubrovnik bound for Korčula make stops at Ston and Orebić three times a day, but to explore the peninsula properly, a rental car is recommended.

SIGHTS & ATTRACTIONS

Orebić

With its history as a trade centre for 500 years, Orebić has a colourful seafaring past and was once quite prosperous, earning money from building ships to supply a merchant fleet. Today, it's a centre for tourism mainly because of its beaches, excellent climate and its proximity to a number of hiking trails. There are some attractions, like the 15th-century **Franjevački Samostan** (Franciscan Monastery) that is located about a 20-minute walk out of town, with its famous (and allegedly miraculous) icon, *Gospa od Angela* (*Our Lady of the Angels*). It was believed the icon would protect mariners from shipwreck, and there are numerous votive offerings from sailors and sea captains who believe it was the Lady who saved their lives.

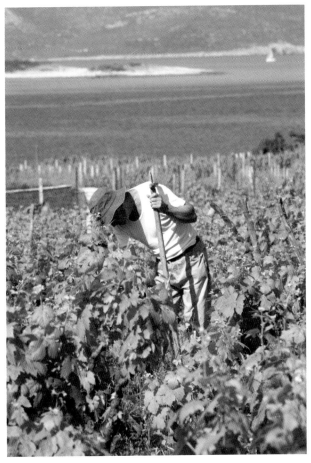

◆ *Excellent wines are produced on the peninsula*

There is also a Virgin and Child by Nikola Firentinac, the 15th-century Renaissance master, who also designed the dome at Šibenik Cathedral. There's a great view of the Pelješac Channel from the monastery terrace.

STON – DEFINITELY WORTH ITS SALT

This fortified town has a split personality: **Mali Ston** is on the north coast and **Veliki Ston** on the south coast. The most impressive feature in Veliki Ston (sometimes called simply Ston) are 14th-century walls that were built to defend Dubrovnik's northern borders. These stretch across a rugged hillside. Ston doesn't look like much at first glance because rebuilding has been slow since the 1996 earthquake, but this small village attracts visitors and people from Dubrovnik en route to Korčula. They come to eat the fresh, succulent oysters produced in Mali Ston Bay that are prepared in a dozen and one ways, from raw and slippery to baked in delicate sauces. While oysters take top billing, restaurants feature ultra-fresh fish dinners as well.

Historically, Ston's major importance was as a salt-producer: when Napoleon invaded Dubrovnik he was as keen to get control of Ston's salt as he was to occupy Dubrovnik. Twenty of the original forty towers along the fortifying walls – and 5 km (3 miles) of the walls themselves – are still standing, and from the top you can get great views of Mljet. There are some interesting Gothic and Renaissance houses here too.

About a 15-minute walk away is Mali Ston. It doesn't have a beach, but you can swim in the clear water from the jetty or rocks. To the north there's a ruined fortress with steps leading to a parapet and great views.

AFTER DARK

RESTAURANTS
Restaurant Mlinica ££ Nice place for a nibble, on the ground floor of the Ostrea hotel (see page 108). ❶ (020) 754 555 Ⓦ www.ostrea.hr

Vila Koruna ££ Both a hotel and a splendid restaurant right on the water. It serves oysters and seafood freshly chosen from stone tanks that sit under the plate-glass windows on the covered terrace of the restaurant. The owner is very friendly and a simple meal can easily turn into an evening party with dancing. It's the oldest eating spot in the region, with oysters, mussels and lobster as its speciality. ⓐ Pelješki put 1, Mali Ston ❶ (020) 754 999 Ⓦ www.vila-koruna.hr

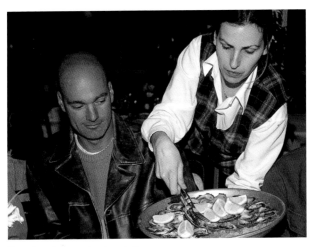

● *Fresh oysters are a local speciality*

Kapetanova Kuća ££–£££ On the waterfront of Mali Ston, this was once the residence of a captain of the guards. Good seafood menu and a wide selection of wines. ① (020) 754 555 Ⓦ www.ostrea.hr

NIGHTLIFE

There's not usually much evening entertainment during the week – aside from the local colour at the hotels and restaurants – but Veliki Ston has concerts and other festivities on weekends. Check with the tourist bureau to find out what's on the agenda.

ACCOMMODATION

Bellevue ££ The hotel sits in a pine wood just 20 m (22 yds) from a pebble beach and has a pool, restaurant and pizzeria. ⓐ Sv Križ 103, Orebić ① (020) 713 193 Ⓦ www.orebic-htp.hr

Orsan ££ A 3-star hotel surrounded by pine and cypress trees on a quiet, sandy bay just a short distance from the sea. ⓐ Bana Jelačića 119 ① (020) 713 193 Ⓦ www.orebic-htp.hr

Ostrea ££ Classed as a family-owned 3-star hotel, the nine rooms on offer are more upmarket than others on the peninsula – even including a 'Presidential Suite'. The hotel also has two good restaurants with a mouthwatering selection of seafood from starters to main (check out the menu on the web). ⓐ Mali Ston ① (020) 754 555 Ⓦ www.ostrea.hr

● *Croatia boasts more than 2,000 km (1,250 miles) of spectacular coastline*

OUT OF TOWN
trips

Split

Split is a place that oozes atmosphere: little wonder, given that this major city actually grew out of a Roman emperor's palatial retirement home. Begun in AD 295, it took Emperor Diocletian ten years to build. The 'court' included living quarters for courtiers, a garrison to guard them, and soldiers to man the garrison. In total the fortified site measured 4,500 sq m (5,382 sq yds); the luxurious apartments of the palace were surrounded by lush gardens. After Diocletian died and left his mini-empire, a succession of despots gradually ran the palace into the ground over the next couple of centuries, until refugees fleeing barbarian invasions moved in and began to restore it.

Modern Split is the second-biggest city in Croatia, with some 220,000 inhabitants and tourism as its major industry. Many of these tourists come for the carnival season, when masked revellers take over the streets for the Feast of St Domnius in May. St Domnius is the city's protector (and patron saint of talented woodworkers), so the markets are full of craftsmen selling their wares during feast days. Split is a lively and friendly city; although it was not bombarded during the 1991 war, it did suffer from the huge influx of refugees and there was a big drop in tourism. Nowadays the visitors have returned. The **Split Tourist Information Office** (📍 Peristil bb 📞 (021) 345 606 🌐 www.visitsplit.com 🕐 08.00–20.30 Mon–Sat, 08.00–13.00 Sun (summer); 08.00–20.00 Mon–Fri, 08.00–13.00 Sat, closed Sun (winter)) is adjacent to the cathedral on the Peristil and here you can find maps of the city, ferry schedules and current phone numbers and addresses for local attractions, eating places, accommodation and so on. The office also sells the **Split Card**, which permits free entry or a discount for museums and galleries plus discounts on car hire, hotels and restaurants.

Central Split

| 0 | 50 metres |
| 0 | 50 yards |

KAVANJINOVA

ZRINJSKO - FRANKOPANSKA

MANDEROVA

ZORANIĆEVA

DOBRI

BIHAČKA

DOMOVINSKOG RATA

Arheološki Muzej

SVAČIĆEVA

METODOVA

BRIBIRSKA

SVAČIĆEVA

KLIŠKA

LIVANJSKA

ISTARSKA

ČAJKOVSKOG

KNINSKA

CRET

PORINOVA

Croatian National Theatre

Franciscan Monastery

KAČIĆEVA

SREDMANUŠKA ❼

TEUTINA

TRG GAJE F BULATA

SINJSKA

MATOŠIĆA

NODILOVA

ZAGREBAČKA

❶

❸ ❺

KRALJA TOMISLAVA

BANA JELAČIĆA

Prokurative

MARMONTOVA

NIGEROVA

COSMUEVA

KRUŽIĆEVA

Grgur Ninski statue

Strossmayerov Park

KRALJA TOMISLAVA

TRG REPUBLIKE

GRAD

DOMALDOVA

SV. MARIJE

KRALJ OBROV

❻

Ribarnica Fish Market

ZADARSKA

SUBIĆEVA

Town Hall

NARODNI TRG

MAJSTORA JURJA

DIOKLECIJANOVA

Zlatna Vrata

CARRARINA POLJANA

Pomorski Muzej

Galerija Meštrović, Marjan & Sustipan

DOBRIĆ

Deljezna Vrata

KRESIMIROVA

BALBONTOVA

DOMINISOVA

PAPALIĆEVA

Muzej Grada

Dioklecijanova Palača

PERISTIL

POLJANA KRALJICE JELENE

Šrebrena Vrata

HRVOJEVA

RIVA (OBALA HRVATSKOG NARODNOG PREPORODA)

BRAĆE RADIĆA

MIHOVILOVA ŠIRINA

i

❷

Katedrala Sv Dujma

Ethnographic Museum

STARI PAZAR

Pazar market

Mjedna Vrata

❹

Harbour

OBALA LAZARETA

OBALA KNEZA DOMAGOJA

ZAGREBAČKA

Legend:
- POI
- ✝ Cathedral
- *i* Information
- 🚆 Railway Stn
- 🚌 Bus Station

N

🚆 ❽ ❾ ❿

Ferry Terminal, Bačvice beach

GETTING THERE

By air
Airlines fly regularly from Dubrovnik (see Ⓦ www.croatiaairlines.com).

By road
There are frequent buses from Dubrovnik; the journey takes about 4¹/₂ hours and is best booked in advance. The bus station is just southeast of the city centre (ⓐ Obala Kneza Domagoja 12, Split ⓣ (060) 327 777 Ⓦ www.ak-split.hr).

By water

In the summer there are ferry connections between Korčula, Hvar (Stari Grad) and Split.

SIGHTS & ATTRACTIONS

Beaches

Locals usually journey out to the islands when they want to swim and enjoy the sunshine, but the main city beach at Bačvice is clean

🔽 *The skyline of Split boasts a dynamic mix of ancient and new*

and you can rent a sunbed and an umbrella there. There are also toilets, showers and bars near the beach. At Bene, on the Marjan Peninsula, there are some rocky coves and shady spots, plus showers and a refreshment bar.

Djoklecijanova Palača (Diocletian's Palace)

For visitors, the main attraction is the Old Town, encircled by town walls with Diocletian's Roman palace at its heart. It's hard to get an image of what the palace must have looked like in the 4th century, since so much of it has been built around and incorporated into the Old Town centre. Little remains of the imperial apartments, although the medieval structures that took their place were built of the stone

🔺 *Diocletian's magnificent palace lies at the heart of Split*

DIOCLETIAN: EGOMANIAC EMPEROR

The Emperor Diocletian enjoyed pursuing grandiose plans and had a limitless passion for building; his constructions included basilicas, circuses, a mint, an arms factory and lots of grand houses for his relatives. Another of his major projects was the Diocletian Baths in Rome, a massive bathing establishment that was to become the largest and most luxurious bath complex in the Empire. Over a period of five years starting in AD 300, more than 10,000 Christian prisoners were used as forced labour to construct the massive edifice that was to accommodate 3,000 bathers with hot, cold and steam baths, plus dressing rooms, gyms, meeting rooms, libraries and gardens. Marble façades graced the exterior and inside mosaic floors were part of a huge structure.

The emperor was born as the son of slaves in Dalmatia, possibly growing up in Salona. He rose up through the ranks in the Roman military and became emperor in AD 284 at the age of 39. Among his positive achievements were that he brought some stability and direction to a Roman Empire already under pressure from barbarian incursions. In an attempt to ensure the continuation of the empire, he created a system of parcelling out authority for the empire, dividing it into four regions, each separately ruled by an emperor. The power-sharing system soon disintegrated once he 'retired', however, and in fact led to his family's downfall. On the less savoury side, Diocletian is also remembered for his ruthless persecution of Christians: many of the country's saints were martyred at his command.

used in the palace. What used to be Diocletian's mausoleum now stands as **Katedrala Sv Dujma** (Cathedral of St Domnius ⓐ Kraj Sv Duje 5), and the baptistery was once a temple. During the period between World War I and World War II, this whole area was badly run down and filled with émigrés and red-light bars – today, it's once again the centre of things, with lots of shops and tourists.

For anyone interested in Roman structures, there are maps available of the original palace and lots of detailed information on the temple, the cathedral, the underground chambers, the peristyle and the many altars. You can enter the area via one of four gates: Zlatna Vrata (Golden Gate), Deljezna Vrata (Iron Gate), Šrebrena Vrata (Silver Gate) and Mjedna Vrata (Bronze Gate).

Marjan

This nature reserve is located on a compact peninsula and is planted with a green assortment of Aleppo pines, cypresses, rosemary and holm oak. From Vidilica, there's a path along the south side of Marjan that leads to the 13th-century Romanesque church of Sv Nikola and the 15th-century church of Sv Jere, built on the remains of an ancient temple.

Pazar & Ribarnica (food markets)

The colourful open-air fruit and vegetable market of Pazar stands just outside the palace walls and is open every day. Since the people of Split haven't totally succumbed to supermarkets, this is where they shop for fresh produce. Photographers love the market and its wildly colourful assortment of peppers, tomatoes, melons, grapes, pomegranates and other delicacies. The Ribarnica (covered fish market) is nearby. ⓐ Just east of Peristil, the Šrebrena Vrata leads on to Pazar ⓛ 07.00–13.00 Mon–Sat, 07.00–11.00 Sun

Sustipan

For quiet walks, the cypress gardens of Sustipan have wonderful views to the sea and Split, plus some park benches on which to rest, to exchange news or to meditate. You can see the foundations of an

◯ *The idyllic gardens of Sustipan*

early medieval church called Sv Stipe (St Stephen) here in the remains
of a Benedictine monastery. In the centre of the gardens stands
a 19th-century neoclassical pavilion.

CULTURE

Arheološki Muzej (Archaeological Museum)

Founded in 1820, this is a well-displayed collection of Roman,
Illyrian, Greek and medieval artefacts that includes jewellery,
amulets, ceramics, glassware and coins. (Don't miss the lewd
oil lamp!) Outside, in an arcaded courtyard and garden, there
are pieces of decorative sculpture, sarcophagi and early Christian
stelae. ⓐ Zrinsko-Frankopanska 25 ⓣ (021) 329 340 ⓛ 09.00–14.00,
16.00–20.00 Mon–Sat, closed Sun (summer); 09.00–14.00,
16.00–20.00 Mon–Fri, 09.00–14.00 Sat, closed Sun (winter)

Galerija Meštrović (Meštrović Gallery)

This monumental villa, built in the early 1930s, was chosen
by Ivan Meštrović, the famous Croatian sculptor, as a summer
residence and studio. He lived here until he fled the country during
World War II. There are almost 200 sculptures on display, both inside
the villa and outside in the gardens, in wood, marble, stone and
bronze, and dating from the beginning of the century to 1946.
ⓐ Šetalište Ivana Meštrovića 46 ⓣ (021) 340 800 ⓦ www.
mestrovic.hr ⓛ 09.00–19.00 Tues–Sun, closed Mon (summer);
09.00–16.00 Tues–Sat, 10.00–15.00 Sun, closed Mon (winter)

Pomorski Muzej (Maritime Museum)

Divided into two sections – naval war and naval trading – this museum
is intriguing even for non-sailors. There are model ships done to scale,

🔺 *The Meštrović Gallery houses works by the famed sculptor*

naval paintings and lots of sailing equipment. Of special interest are the world's first self-propelled torpedoes. Designed by Ivan Blaž Lupis, a Croat, and developed in conjunction with the British engineer Robert Whitehead, the model was successfully trialled in 1866.
🅐 Glagoljaška 18 ☎ (021) 347 788 🆆 www.hpms.hr 🕐 09.00–21.00 Mon–Fri, 09.00–17.00 Sat, closed Sun (summer); 09.30–14.30 Mon–Wed & Fri, 09.30–14.30, 17.00–20.00 Thur, 09.00–13.00 Sat, closed Sun (winter)

RETAIL THERAPY

For those who like antiques shops, **Antique** (ⓐ Cosmijeva 1 ⓣ (021) 362 315 ⓦ www.antique-impex.hr ⓛ 09.00–20.00 Mon–Fri, 09.00–13.00 Sat, closed Sun) and **Zlatna Vrata** (ⓐ Carrarina poljana 1 ⓣ (021) 360 122 ⓛ 09.00–12.30, 17.00–20.00 Mon–Fri, 09.00–13.00 Sat, closed Sun) are worth a browse. For handicrafts, the market in the cellars of Diocletian's Palace has a good assortment.

For high-quality Croatian wines, honey, olive oils and truffles, check out **Judita Gourmet & Wine** (ⓐ Marulićeva 1 ⓣ (021) 210 250 ⓦ www.stella-croatica.hr ⓛ 08.30–22.00 daily). More Croatian wines are found at **Vinoteka Bouquet** (ⓐ Trg dr Franje Tuđmana 3, off Trg Republike ⓣ (021) 348 031 ⓦ www.vinoteka.hr ⓛ 08.30–12.30, 17.00–20.30 Mon–Fri, 09.00–13.30 Sat, closed Sun). For plain, everyday fare of great quality such as *rakija*, buns and cakes and wine, it is best to go to the market east of Šrebrena Vrata (Silver Gate). The best place to buy snacks and fresh food is the daily market at the eastern edge of the Old Town, where you can pick up the ingredients for a picnic – hams, cheeses, tomatoes, lettuce, olives, etc. If you need a bigger range of goods, the **Gavrilović** supermarket (ⓐ Obala Kneza Domagoja ⓛ 07.00–23.00 daily) is perched at the ferry terminal. The bakery **Prerada** (ⓐ Kamila Tončića 3 ⓣ (021) 347 738 ⓛ 06.00–20.00 daily) intoxicates with its freshly baked breads, cakes and strudels.

TAKING A BREAK

Babić £ ❶ This is a good place for a takeaway pizza slice, the omnipresent and delicious *pršut*, sandwiches and pastries. ⓐ Marmontova 7 ⓛ 11.00–24.00 daily

Bobis £ ❷ For those with a sweet tooth, Bobis has a large café on the Riva strip and a smaller outlet on Marmontova. ⓐ Riva (Obala hrvatskog narodnog preporoda) 20 ⓣ (021) 347 962 ⓛ 06.00–22.00 Mon–Sat, 07.00–22.00 Sun

Kantun Paulina £ ❸ This is the place to get *ćevapčići*, a kind of spicy meat rissole beloved by the Croatians for snack food. ⓐ Matošića 1 ⓣ (021) 395 973 ⓛ 08.00–23.30 Mon–Sat, 10.00–23.30 Sun

Kuća sladoleda Ivona £ ❹ Croatian ice cream can be found in many outlets but some of the best is here. ⓐ Riva (Obala hrvatskog narodnog preporoda) 25 ⓣ (021) 345 311 ⓦ www.tangar.hr ⓛ 08.00–23.00 daily (summer); 12.00–20.00 Mon, 09.00–21.00 Tues–Sun (winter)

AFTER DARK

RESTAURANTS

For a tourist town there's a curious shortage of high-quality restaurants in the Old Town, but there are a few outside the city walls. A good area to check out is on the western edge of the Old Town in the lanes west of Trg Republike. Restaurants tend to stay open until 23.00 or 24.00.

Pizzeria Galija £ ❺ Excellent pizza cooked in a charcoal oven plus lots of pasta and antipasti. ⓐ Tončićeva 12, a block north of Trg Republike ⓣ (021) 347 932 ⓛ 09.00–23.30 Mon–Sat, 12.00–23.30 Sun

Zlatna Ribica £ ❻ Right by the fish market, a stand-up buffet with cheap seafood snacks that are chalked on to a blackboard. ⓐ Kraj Sv Marije 12 ⓣ (021) 348 710 ⓛ 06.00–22.00 daily (summer); 06.00–21.00 Mon–Fri, 06.00–14.00 Sat & Sun (winter)

Konoba Kod Joze ££ ❼ This cosy and intimate restaurant with fish nets on the wall is considered one of the best seafood restaurants in Split. Its risottos and pastas are good. ❸ Sredmanuška 4 (heading north through Strossmayerov Park, this street is on the right) ❶ (021) 347 397 ❺ 10.00–24.00 Mon–Fri, 12.00–24.00 Sat & Sun

🔺 *Downtown dining in Split*

Stellon ££ ❽ In a country whose restaurants do mainly fish and meat, Stellon is a good option for vegetarians with its hearty salads and pasta and veggie mains. Smart, slick, hyper-modern interior but reasonably priced. ⓐ Preradovićevo šetalište bb ⓣ (021) 489 200 ⓛ 08.00–01.00 Tues–Sun, closed Mon (summer); 10.00–01.00 Tues–Sun, closed Mon (winter)

Boban £££ ❾ For a gourmet meal, this is the number-one choice – as it has been for such luminaries as Placido Domingo. Croatian dishes are given an Italian twist in a nod to fusion cuisine with lobster done up as a spicy tomato stew and a fish carpaccio done sushi-style. Great wine list. ⓐ Hektorovićeva 49, parallel to Bačvice beach road Put Firula ⓣ (021) 543 300 ⓛ 10.00–24.00 Mon–Fri, 12.00–24.00 Sat & Sun

Šumica £££ ❿ The emphasis here is on presenting the freshest possible fish and shellfish, but there are other choices on the menu such as a sophisticated version of the omnipresent schnitzel. The 'smart set' hangs out in this classy restaurant with its big outdoor terrace. ⓐ Put Firula 6 ⓣ (021) 389 897 ⓛ 12.00–23.00 daily

BARS, CLUBS & DISCOS

For what's playing, check the town website (ⓦ www.visitsplit.com), tourist information, the newspaper *Slobodna Dalmacija* or municipal posters displayed on billboards throughout the Old Town. These will also announce numerous open-air pop concerts that are held during the summer months. The nightlife scene in Split is not wild; it is particularly quiet in the summer, when a lot of people leave town for the islands.

Club Sing Sing This is a club at ground level, which plays Croatian pop and rock, with occasional cover bands. It's a 15-minute walk from the Old Town. ⓐ Preradovićevo šetalište bb (Bačvice) 🕐 09.00–02.00 daily (summer); 09.00–24.00 Mon–Thur, 09.00–06.00 Fri & Sat, closed Sun (winter)

Ghetto Club Tables pepper an outdoor courtyard in summer – there are occasional exhibitions and performances for the alternative crowd. ⓐ Dosud 10, near Marulićeva 🕐 10.00–02.00 Fri & Sat, 10.00–01.00 Sun–Thur (summer); 16.00–02.00 Fri & Sat, 16.00–01.00 Sun–Thur (winter)

Hemingway Dress to impress at Split's most glamorous club and cocktail bar, right on the main city beach, north of the centre near the Poljud stadium. ⓐ Osmih Mediteranskih igara 5 ☎ 099 211 9933 (mobile) 🕐 08.00–06.00 daily

Kocka An alternative club with a mixed programme of films, DJ nights and live gigs. In summer, opens for special events only. ⓐ Savska bb (under Mažuranićevo šetalište in the Youth Centre, a 15-minute walk northeast of the Old Town) ☎ (021) 540 537 ⓦ www.kocka.hr

Puls2 A trendy bar where the hip clientele can be found draped over comfy lounge chairs. On Fridays, there's live music. ⓐ Buvnina 1, near Marulićeva 🕐 08.00–02.00 Mon–Sat, 16.00–01.00 Sun

Quasimodo Just north of the centre, this is the city's prime address for live music: rock'n'roll, jazz, blues and more by local and regional bands. ⓐ Gundulićeva 26 🕐 07.00–03.00 Mon–Sat, closed Sun

ACCOMMODATION

Jupiter £ With double, triple and quad rooms with shared bathrooms in the hallway. It's a friendly place in a good location. @ Grabovčeva širina 1 ① (021) 344 801 ⓦ www.hotel-jupiter.info

Adriana ££ Small, very comfortable hotel with modern double rooms right above a seafront café-pizzeria. @ Riva (Obala hrvatskog narodnog preporoda) 8 ① (021) 340 000 ⓦ www.hotel-adriana.com

Bellevue Hotel ££ Overlooking the sea; comfortable and convenient if not stylish. @ Bana Jelačića 2, off Trg Republike ① (021) 345 644 ⓦ www.hotel-bellevue-split.hr

Consul ££ On a quiet street near the Old Town with comfortable, modern rooms and a terrace. @ Tršćanska 34 ① (021) 340 130 ⓦ www.hotel-consul.net

Park ££ This has been a hotel since 1921 and has an exclusive feel to it. The rooms are smartly decorated and there is a good restaurant. @ Hatzeov perivoj 3 ① (021) 406 400 ⓦ www.hotelpark-split.hr

President ££ Lots of facilities with plush rooms and apartments, this 4-star property is a five-minute walk north of the Old Town. @ Starčevićeva 1 ① (021) 305 222 ⓦ www.hotelpresident.hr

Vestibul Palace £££ A beautiful modern hotel in the heart of Split's old palace quarter. Rooms have Roman, Gothic and Renaissance brickwork, and there's an impressive atrium. @ Iza Vestibula 4, near Bronze Gate ① (021) 329 329 ⓦ http://vestibulpalace.com

Hvar

This is one of the most beautiful and popular islands in Croatia, so it attracts tour groups from all over Europe. The capital, Hvar Town, has a 16th-century Venetian air, there are excellent beaches and the weather (according to fans) is sunnier and warmer than elsewhere. Locals insist there are 2,700 hours of sunshine a year and snow is rare. The main crop on the island is lavender and it's on sale everywhere – come in the spring and the air is heady with the scent. Wine is also produced, along with figs and olives.

Hvar Town, with its well-preserved Venetian Renaissance architecture, easily challenges Korčula and Dubrovnik in beauty, although the summer crowds can be a bit much. It's better to visit in the spring or autumn. The town wraps itself around a bay (Luca Hvar) and the main square, Trg Sv Stjepana, which is allegedly the biggest main square in Dalmatia. Beyond the town, stone houses clamber up three hills to a peak crowned by a Venetian fortress. After Dubrovnik, this is probably the most fashionable of Adriatic resorts for Croats, who love to sit in the cafés of the main square. ⓦ www.hvar.hr

GETTING THERE

By water

The best travel links are to Split, with regular ferry connections from Stari Grad. **Jadrolinija** (ⓣ (051) 666 111 ⓦ www.jadrolinija.hr) runs a daily catamaran service that also stops at Hvar Town on its way to and from the island of Lastovo to Split. From Dubrovnik it is easiest to hire a car and cross on the ferry that runs from the mainland at Drvenik to Sućuraj on the eastern tip of the island. There are also links to Korčula in the south and thence to Dubrovnik.

SIGHTS & ATTRACTIONS

Benediktinski Samostan (Benedictine Convent)

This is small as convents go, but the nuns here spend their time making the extraordinary Hvar lace, which is sold in shops in Hvar Town. The nuns never leave the grounds and are bound by an oath of silence.
⊘ Northwest of Trg Sv Stjepana ❶ (021) 741 052 ⏱ 10.00–12.00, 17.00–19.00 Mon–Fri (June–Aug); closed Sat, Sun & Sept–May

Biskupska Riznica (The Bishop's Treasury)

Next door to the cathedral, this holds a small collection of reliquaries, embroidery and chalices. ⊘ Trg Sv Stjepana bb ❶ (021) 741 269 ⏱ 09.00–12.00, 17.00–19.00 daily

Španjola (Citadel)

Built in the 1550s by the Venetians (aided by Spanish engineers), the building is called Španjola locally. Inside, there's a marine archaeology collection and a display of amphorae and Greco-Roman drinking vessels. The biggest attraction is the view from the ramparts.

Palača Hektorović (Hektorović Palace)

On the north side of the main square, this is a slightly spooky house that was left unfinished when it was built in the 15th century. Named after a famous poet, it has Venetian Gothic windows, and is one of the best examples of Venetian architecture on the island. ⊘ Northwest of Trg Sv Stjepana

Katedrala Sv Stjepana (St Stephen's Cathedral)

As a backdrop to the main square, this basilica was built between the 16th and 17th centuries on the foundations of an earlier Benedictine

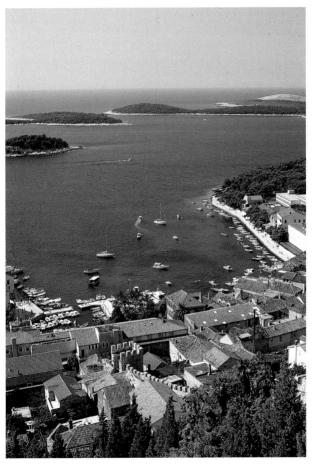

⬛ *The Pakleni Islands lie off the coast of Hvar*

THE ARSENAL – DRAMA FROM A CRISIS

This hulking 17th-century arcaded building dominates the square. It was where war galleys were once hauled out to be repaired. In 1612, the upper floor was converted into a theatre; it is the oldest in Croatia and one of the first in Europe. Check out the inscription inside – 'Anno Secundo Pacis MDCXII': this refers to the peace after a century-long quarrel between commoners and aristocrats. It followed an uprising in 1510 when 19 men were hanged from galley masts. The theatre was built to calm the distrust between nobles and commoners, since both classes shared theatrical space. ❷ Trg Sv Stjepana

monastery and even earlier 6th-century church. It has a Renaissance trefoil façade and a lovely campanile; inside, you can admire the 13th-century Madonna and Child. ❷ Trg Sv Stjepana

Trg Sv Stjepana (St Stephen's Square)

Dating back to the 13th century, this imposing square opens on to the Mandrac, an enclosed harbour for small boats that leads to a larger bay. The old buildings lining the square have been converted into restaurants, galleries and small cafés.

AFTER DARK

RESTAURANTS

There's a full range of eating places in Hvar. Grilled fish and meat and black risotto are on offer, as ever, but local specialities include Dalmatian stewed beef, fritters, fig torte and octopus salad.

Bounty £–££ Grilled fish and meat with the mandatory seafood risottos. Try the excellent fish soup and the white house wine. ❷ Fabrika, on the inner harbour ❶ (021) 742 565 ❸ 10.00–24.00 daily (summer); 10.00–15.00, 18.00–22.00 daily (winter)

Macondo ££–£££ A first-class fish restaurant with faultless food and service – but be prepared to wait for a table. It boasts a small terrace for summer dining and a large open fire for colder nights. ❷ Groda, in a narrow alley between the main square and the fortress ❶ (021) 742 850 ❸ 12.00–23.00 daily

BARS

Carpe Diem Trendy cocktail bar that attracts all the 'beautiful people', so you'll be among friends. It overlooks the sea and has oriental wicker furniture and a plant-filled terrace. ❷ Obala oslobođenja ❶ (021) 742 369 ❿ www.carpe-diem-hvar.com

Carpe Diem Beach Party all night at Carpe Diem's stylish island beach club, reached by taxi-boats from town. ❷ Stipanska beach, Marinkovac Island ❿ www.carpe-diem-beach.com ❸ 12.00–05.00 daily (summer); closed winter

Loco On the main square, this is the best of the youth-oriented bars in town. Stylish, relaxing and chic. ❷ Trg Sv Stjepana ❶ (021) 742 625 ❸ 08.00–02.00 daily (summer); 08.00–24.00 daily (winter)

Veneranda Set in and around a former Greek church a few minutes' walk west of the centre, this all-night dancing venue has concerts, DJs, film projections and nice views over town. ❷ Gornja cesta bb ❿ www.veneranda.hr ❸ 22.00–05.00 daily (summer); closed winter

ACCOMMODATION

Local hoteliers have joined forces in order to try to lure visitors in the winter months: free board and lodging if the temperatures go below freezing during the day, and 50 per cent off if it rains for more than three hours during the day. Whether travelling in the summer or the winter, it's a good idea to book rooms on Hvar well in advance. See Ⓦ www.suncanihvar.com for additional hotel information.

Dalmacija £ A basic but comfortable 2-star hotel on the seafront, near the centre. ⓐ Obala Ivana Lučića-Lavčevića ⓣ (021) 741 120

Boškinac ££ Eight elegant rooms in a beautifully renovated old building, with a restaurant and tavern downstairs. ⓐ Novaljsko polje bb ⓣ (053) 663 500 Ⓦ www.boskinac.com ⓑ Mar–Dec

Palace Hotel ££ This 76-room 'palace', built during the Habsburg era, sits on the edge of the main square overlooking the harbour. Amenities include two restaurants, an outdoor seawater pool, massage room and sauna. ⓐ Trg Sv Stjepana ⓣ (021) 741 966 ⓦ www.suncanihvar.com

Podstine ££ This is a quiet, family-run hotel near a pebble beach about 20 minutes west of the main square. Seventeen rooms, each with a sea view and a lovely terrace restaurant. ⓐ Podstine bb ⓣ (021) 740 400 ⓦ www.podstine.com ⓛ May–Oct

Slavia Hotel ££ A 3-star, three-storey hotel with en-suite rooms near the ferry dock. Breakfast is served on a terrace right by the harbour. ⓐ Obala oslobođenja ⓣ (021) 741 820

● *Lavender is the main crop on Hvar*

Pag

In any island beauty contest, Pag wouldn't even be a contender, but it does have qualities that make it well worth visiting. The island lies in the south of the Kvarner Gulf and is a stark and desolate place that looks like it couldn't possibly support any form of life. A small population (and three times as many sheep) do live there, however, and they produce two things that have made the islanders famous throughout Croatia – cheese and lace. Pag cheese is a hard, piquant sheep's cheese known as *paški sir* that tastes like a cross between old cheddar and Parmesan. Its distinctive taste comes from a mixture of olive oil and ash that is rubbed into the cheese before it's left to mature and from the wild herbs (like sage) and the salty vegetation that the sheep eat. The cheese tends to be a bit expensive but it's well worth the price. Pag lamb is also delicious, with the same wild herb taste.

GETTING THERE

By road
The Rijeka to Zadar bus passes through Novalja and Pag Town twice daily in each direction.

By water
There is a bridge linking the south of the island to the mainland, and a ferry from Karlobag on the mainland to Pag Town.

SIGHTS & ATTRACTIONS

Beaches
The three main beaches are Straško, Zrče and Časka.

Novalja

This developed resort lies close to several good beaches, so it attracts resort-seeking tourists and the all-night party crowd. Zrče beach, 2 km (1¼ miles) south of Novalja, has become one of Croatia's hottest spots at night in the summer with clubs that stay open until dawn. The major historical attraction nearby is the Roman town of Cissa or Časka (largely underwater) but there is an underground aqueduct with sections that you can visit. You enter through the town museum, whose collection includes amphorae from a 1st-century Roman ship.

Pag Town

This is the administrative centre for the island and there's a mix of new and old. The town was actually established in the 15th century and has a medieval quality. The parish church of **Sv Marije** (❷ Trg Kralja

PAG LACE

Lace is Pag's most famous industry, and a craft that remains very traditional and non-commercial. Once prized by emperors as 'white gold', 'Pag lace' is a relatively new name. The work is painstaking and created using an ordinary darning needle; each piece is unique and done without a draft or plan. When it is finished it is firm, as if starched, and will stay that way even after washing. While you can buy Pag lace in shops in Dubrovnik, it's a special experience to purchase it directly from the women dressed in local costume who sit on stools outside their homes. Women dressed in black come into town as well in the mornings to sell their handicraft.

Petra Kresmira IV) is worth a visit, if only to see the rose window on the Gothic church façade that resembles the intricate pattern used in local lace. In Pag Town, there's a tiny **Lace Museum** (ⓐ Kralja Svonimira), just off the main square.

AFTER DARK

RESTAURANTS

Taverna Boškanić £–££ Looking down on Stara Novalja, this is where to meet locals over wine and great platters of *pršut*, *paški sir* and sardines. ⓐ Novaljsko polje bb ⓣ (053) 663 500 ⓛ 12.00–24.00 daily (Mar–Dec); closed Jan & Feb

Natale ££ Right near the harbour in Pag Town, this restaurant specialises in Pag lamb and seafood – and also great *palačinke* and pizzas. ⓐ Stjepana Radića 2 ⓣ (023) 611 194

Restaurant Steffani ££ This is in the heart of Novalja and very popular with the locals as well as visitors. The usual seafood and lamb along with some local specialities like snails. ⓐ Škopljanska 20 ⓣ (053) 661 697

Biser ££–£££ This hotel restaurant has a terrace overlooking the sea and serves local fare, seafood and other Croatian specialities. ⓐ A G Matoša 8 ⓣ (023) 611 333 ⓦ www.hotel-biser.com ⓛ 07.00–24.00 daily

NIGHTLIFE

Novalja (see page 135) is where the action is and where young people head if they're looking for dancing, drinking, eating and socialising outdoors until the wee hours of the morning. There are a variety of clubs right on the beaches, so the party spills out on to the sand as DJs spin the latest in dance tracks. Each of the beaches has its following, but everyone's favourite, and the Novalja hotspot, is Zrče beach.

ACCOMMODATION

Biser ££ On a good beach in Pag Town, en-suite rooms (some with sea views), TV and air conditioning. ⓐ A G Matoša 8 ⓣ (023) 611 333 ⓦ www.hotel-biser.com

Pagus Hotel ££ On a small beach and central, the Pagus has spacious en-suite rooms. ⓐ Ante Starčevića 1 ⓣ (023) 611 310 ⓦ www.coning-turizam.hr/pagus

Plaža £££ The 4-star Plaza in Pag has smart en-suites plus other amenities such as a pool and fitness centre. ⓐ Marka Marulića 14 ⓣ (023) 600 855 ⓦ www.plaza-croatia.com ⓛ June–Sept

○ *Pag Town with its sheltered harbour*

Plitvice Lakes National Park

While this stunning park is closer to Zagreb than it is to Dubrovnik, it is well worth a stop either on the way from the airport in Zagreb or on the way back. It's the country's oldest and largest national park and is on the UNESCO World Heritage list of sites – and little wonder. Sixteen emerald-green lakes spill one into the other via cataracts and waterfalls of varying height; the limestone rock around and in the lakes is a veritable artist's box of colours. The largest waterfall, Veliki Slap, is almost 70 m (230 ft) high. The water in the lakes hits every shade of green and blue and tree-shaded paths border the main lakes. The lakes are set in deep forests still populated by bears, wolves and wild boar, and cover nearly 300 sq km (116 sq miles).

GETTING THERE

By road

Plitvice is about halfway between Zagreb and Zadar on the main road, with regular buses going from each of these and also from Split. There are two entry gates (Ulaz 1 in the north and Ulaz 2 in the south) each providing access to a different section of the lakes. Most of the park's infrastructure (hotels, tourist office, post office, restaurant) are closer to Ulaz 2. Getting back to Dubrovnik or Zagreb is a bit tricky since buses don't always stop, especially if they're full – you need to flag them down.

TAKING A BREAK

Lička Kuća ££ This is a rustic mountain-chalet type of place with wooden tables and chairs that serves traditional Lika food like roast

lamb, spicy sausages and *đuveđ* (ratatouille flavoured with paprika).
ⓐ Rastovača bb, opposite Ulaz 1 ⓣ (053) 751 382 ⓛ 11.00–23.00 daily

ACCOMMODATION

The phenomenon of the private room thrives as an accommodation
option here. These can be booked at the kiosks open in July and August

🔺 *The breathtaking scenery of the Plitvice Lakes National Park*

WATER & WILDLIFE

Veliki Slap literally means 'the Big Waterfall', and big it is. This high wall of water is the park's main attraction and the dramatic focus of the lakes. Other highlights are the largest lake, Kozjak, and Labudovac Falls. The park is also rich in wildlife: alongside the bears and wolves live animals such as lynxes and otters, while birdwatchers can look out for rare species including the eagle, peregrine falcon, hoopoe, capercaillie and eagle owl. There are well-marked paths, walkways and bridges linking the main attractions; alternatively, there are regular park buses and ferries for those who prefer a less strenuous day out.

and run by park authorities at both entry gates, Ulaz 1 and 2. At other times, the tourist office in the nearby village of Korenica will book private rooms (🕿 (053) 776 798 🌐 www.tzplitvice.hr). The tourist office in nearby Rakovica (🕿 (047) 784 450) also handles private room bookings.

Bellevue Hotel ££ Basic, not fancy hotel with seventy rooms (six singles) with en-suite bathrooms. Popular with tour groups.
🅐 Plitvička Jezera, near Ulaz 2 🕿 (053) 751 700 🕐 Apr–Oct

Jezero ££–£££ Built on high ground overlooking the lakes, this is definitely the most luxurious hotel in the park. Resembling a large mountain lodge, there are 210 rooms decorated in natural pinewood. There are tennis courts, a sauna, a bowling alley and a fitness centre.
🅐 Plitvička Jezera 🕿 (053) 751 400

🅞 *Waiting for the catch of the day on Sipan Island*

PRACTICAL
information

PRACTICAL INFORMATION

Directory

GETTING THERE
By air

Flying to Croatia is fast becoming easier and cheaper as more airlines add flights to Zagreb, Split and Dubrovnik, especially in the summer season. Croatia Airlines and British Airways fly direct to Dubrovnik from the UK year round and other carriers, including easyJet and bmibaby, offer direct flights there in summer. Flights from London to Zagreb take just over two hours (and about thirty minutes longer to Dubrovnik). Although BA and Croatia Airlines have reduced fares considerably in recent years, it's possible to get cheaper prices or more convenient connections by doing a little research online to find a budget airline flight. If money is tight, you can even consider using one of these airlines to fly to an airport in a nearby country and then continue on overland. Check connections to Venice, Ljubljana or Tivat in Montenegro.

Travellers from further away (especially from North America, Australia and New Zealand) can dramatically reduce their travel costs by flying into a hub city in Europe with a large airline and then switching to a budget airline from the same airport to travel on to Zagreb, Split or Dubrovnik. Note that these connections are not guaranteed and you'd need to collect baggage, pass through customs and check in again for the next flight – so do leave a few hours for this. Up-to-date budget airline route information can be found at Ⓦ www.whichbudget.com

bmi ❶ 0844 8484 888 Ⓦ www.flybmi.com
British Airways ❶ 0844 493 0787 Ⓦ www.ba.com
Croatia Airlines ❶ (385) (0)1 667 6555 Ⓦ www.croatiaairlines.com
easyJet ❶ 0905 821 0905 Ⓦ www.easyjet.com

Many people are aware that air travel emits CO_2, which contributes to climate change. You may be interested in the possibility of lessening the environmental impact of your flight through the charity **Climate Care**, which offsets your CO_2 by funding environmental projects around the world. Visit ⓦ www.jpmorganclimatecare.com

By rail

Travelling to Dubrovnik by rail is another option if you want to include other cities and travel in a leisurely way, but it's not an inexpensive choice. Rather than buy a return rail ticket to Croatia, it's wiser to invest in a rail pass and plan your own itinerary. There are a huge array of rail passes available, many of which must be bought before leaving home, while others can only be bought in the country for which they are valid. Inter-Rail Passes (available only for European residents) are available for 16 to 22 days or one month, and can be bought to cover two zones or all zones (global pass): 28 countries are grouped into zones. Eurodomino Passes, also only available to European residents, are individual country passes that provide unlimited travel in 25 European and North African countries. The pass allows you anything from three to eight days' extensive travel within a one-month period on the entire rail network of the chosen country.

A useful website for any kind of rail information is **The Man in Seat Sixty-One** (ⓦ www.seat61.com). For **Rail Europe** call ⓣ 0844 8484 064 or check out ⓦ www.raileurope.co.uk

By road

If you're coming by car, the most common road route from the UK to Dubrovnik is to take motorways from the Channel coast via Brussels, Cologne, Frankfurt, Munich, Salzburg and on to Ljubljana. From here take ordinary roads south to Rijeka on the Adriatic and then the coastal road through Split and on to Dubrovnik. Another route would be through France and Switzerland to Italy's Adriatic coast and Bari, from where you can catch the ferry to Dubrovnik. The disadvantage of having a car is that parking in Dubrovnik is difficult and expensive: hotel car parks are full to overflowing and there is almost no street parking. The 'Sanitat Dubrovnik' mounts regular patrols to seek out illegally parked cars and will tow them away to a pound in Lapad.

The cheapest way to get to Croatia from the UK is by bus. Eurolines offers a return ticket daily from London to Zagreb that costs less than £200 and takes less than 31 hours to Zagreb and 37 to Split (two nights are spent on the road). The company also has a pass that links 46 European cities and will get you as far as Vienna – once there, you pay for an additional bus or train ticket to Zagreb or beyond.

Eurolines ☎ 0871 7818 181 in the UK ⓦ www.eurolines.co.uk

By water

There is ferry service to Croatia from several Italian Adriatic ports (Ancona, Bari and Pescara) run by Jadrolinija and SNAV. If you're travelling by car, book well in advance especially in high season; if going on foot, you can usually buy tickets on arrival in Ancona or Bari. During peak travel times, there are also swift hydrofoil and catamaran services between Italian ports and Zadar and Split for passengers only. On overnight trips, you can pay less than £20 for a bed in a basic cabin. For timetables, contact the ferry companies:

Jadrolinija ☎ (385) 51 666 111 ⓦ www.jadrolinija.hr

SNAV ☎ +39 71 207 6116 ⓦ www.snav.it

ENTRY FORMALITIES

Holders of full, valid EU, Canadian, US, Australian and New Zealand passports can enter Croatia without a visa for stays of up to 90 days

(South Africans require a visa, obtainable in Pretoria). For longer stays, visa extensions are available by crossing the border into Italy or Slovenia and then re-entering. Other nationals require a visa for a small fee. Non-EU nationals must provide evidence of sufficient funds (at least £100 per day). Theoretically, all visitors are required to register with the police but this is now a formality handled by the hotel clerks.

There is no duty on non-commercial goods brought in by visitors up to 30,000kn, although it is wise to register very expensive camera equipment or laptops. Also allowed: up to 200 cigarettes, 1 litre of spirits, 2 litres of wine, 500 g of coffee, 250 ml of perfume and up to 15,000kn in currency. For details on the rather complicated arrangements for reimbursement of VAT and other details, see Ⓦ www.carina.hr

For further information on entry formalities check the Croatian government website at Ⓦ www.mvp.hr

MONEY

The main unit of currency is the kuna, which is divided into 100 lipa. Coins come in denominations of 5, 10, 20 and 50 lipa and 1, 2 and 5 kuna. Notes (which depict Croatian heroes) come in denominations of 10, 20, 50, 100, 200, 500 and 1,000 kuna. The currency gets its name from *kuna*, the Croatian word meaning marten – in medieval days taxes were paid in pelts from the animal – and *lipa*, meaning linden tree. The euro is the secondary currency now and the government tries to keep rates of exchange steady. The kuna is not a fully convertible currency, so you will need to buy it when you arrive and exchange it when you leave the country.

In main towns and cities, Automated Teller Machines (ATMs) are available to be used with internationally recognised cards. Check the symbol at the back of your card with those shown on the bankomat.

The kuna is the unit of currency in Croatia

Traveller's cheques can only be exchanged in a bank, and cash advances on American Express cards can be obtained from Atlas travel agency, wherever they have an office. Most commonly used credit cards (Visa, MasterCard, American Express and Diners Club International) are accepted in large shops, hotels, restaurants and resorts and can be used for cash advances in banks.

HEALTH, SAFETY & CRIME

Dubrovnik is a relatively safe destination with most food safe to eat and tap water safe to drink throughout the country. Croatians claim they have the cleanest water in Europe and, looking at the crystal-clear lakes and rivers, you're inclined to believe them.
No inoculations are required for travel to Croatia, but anyone planning to do some trekking in the mountains should investigate being inoculated against tick-borne encephalitis. (Spray generously with tick repellents and wear long trousers tucked into your boots, and a hat.)

There is a reciprocal agreement between Croatia and the EU countries for free healthcare, but sometimes certain services are not available in the public hospitals and you will have to be treated privately. Since private care is not cheap, it's a wise idea to take out health insurance for major emergencies. Small medical problems are usually treated at one of Dubrovnik's pharmacies (*ljekarna*), where there is usually someone who speaks English. Pharmacies operate a rota system, so there's usually one open at night-time and on weekends (check the posting on the window of the pharmacy).

For more serious problems, head for the nearest hospital (*bolnica* or *klinički centar*). Normal hospital treatment is free to citizens of most EU countries on producing a valid passport. Hospitals are clean and well run, although there might be a shortage of Western drugs. The most common complaints seem to be sunburn, seasickness, insect bites and stepping on sea urchin spikes.

Croatia is relatively safe when it comes to crime, but petty theft can occur and the best defence here is common sense. Don't flash around a lot of money, don't carry a wallet in a hip pocket and don't wear expensive jewellery. It's a good idea to take out travel insurance before you leave and take photocopies of all your documents, credit cards, etc. Streets should be reasonably safe at night.

OPENING HOURS

The usual opening hours for shops are 07.00–20.00 Monday to Friday and 08.00–14.00 or 15.00 on Saturday. Food stores such as the supermarkets will generally stay open until 18.00 on Saturday and will open on Sunday mornings as well. Open-air markets are normally open 07.00–13.00 Monday to Saturday and 07.00–11.00 on Sunday. Clothing shops and bookshops are open 09.00–13.00 and 17.00–19.30 Monday to Friday; also 09.00–13.00 on Saturday. These hours may vary in the summer months, particularly in tourist centres. Banks are generally open 08.00–17.00 from Monday to

Friday and 08.00–11.00 or 12.00 on Saturday. Usual hours at post offices are 07.00–19.00 Monday to Friday and 08.00–13.00 or 14.00 on Saturday. Pharmacies are usually open 08.00–19.00 Monday–Friday and 08.00–14.00 Saturday.

TOILETS

Every restaurant and bar will have a toilet, but it's a good idea to cough up for an espresso or drink if you do use their facilities. Public toilets (*zahod* or WC) in town are more difficult to find, but they are usually clean, well stocked and hygienic. In trains and bus stations, the toilets usually come with a small charge of a couple of kuna. Men use facilities marked *Muški* and women's are *Ženski*.

CHILDREN

Croats love children – their own and those of visitors as well. Children tend to stay up late and, instead of being left with a babysitter, will often accompany their parents to a late dinner in a restaurant. Croatian pizzas tend to be close to the originals from Naples and popular with kids. Ice-cream parlours are also popular with children.

The Adriatic waters are clear and fantastic for swimming, but be warned that many beaches are pebbly rather than sandy and there may be sea urchins about, so take jelly beach shoes for non-swimmers or younger children.

Boat trips are another effortless way of entertaining children. Most include lunch and a chance to swim. A trip in a glass-bottom cruise boat is an ideal way of introducing children to the marine life of the area. Check out ⓦ www.korculainfo.com for the best options.

Festivals always provide family fun, particularly those aimed at younger audiences, such as the **Puppet Theatre Festival** in Osijek (ⓐ Children's Theatre Branko Mihaljević) held in early May. Children will also enjoy the Moreška Sword Dance (see page 9), performed through the summer in Korčula.

For visitors on longer stays there are wonderful kids' camps that offer highly creative arts programmes, sailing, language lessons and a lot more – see Ⓦ www.adriatica.net/kids

COMMUNICATIONS
Internet
Using the Internet is especially popular here, so there are plenty of Internet cafés, tourist agency rooms with computers, or sometimes just a lonely computer in the corner of a bar (cost is usually around 5 to 20kn per hour). Top-end hotels have cable lines in the rooms. Some of the Internet venues use a Croatian keyboard, so ask for help – web addresses omit the accents. In Dubrovnik, try:

Hugo ⓐ Prijeko 13 ☏ (020) 322 069 🕐 09.00–23.00 daily (summer); 10.00–20.00 daily (winter)

Internet Bar 'NETCAFE' ⓐ Prijeko 21 ☏ (020) 321 025 🕐 09.00–01.00 daily (summer); 09.00–23.00 daily (winter)

Internet Club & Call Shop Snoopy ⓐ Bana Jelačića 33 ☏ (020) 312 274 🕐 09.00–23.00 Mon–Sat, 13.00–23.00 Sun (summer); 10.00–23.00 Mon–Sat, 13.00–23.00 Sun (winter)

Phone
Public phones use magnetic cards called *telefonska kartica* and these can be purchased at newspaper kiosks or post offices. Rates change according to the time you call, with peak times at 07.00–22.00; Sunday has a 50 per cent discount. For local directory enquiries call ☏ 11888; international directory enquiries ☏ 11802 and for weather ☏ 18166 or road help and conditions ☏ 1987

TELEPHONING CROATIA

To call Croatia from abroad you should dial your exit code
(00 or other) followed by the Croatia country code (385),
then 20 plus the local number for all Dubrovnik numbers.

TELEPHONING ABROAD

For the best rates, go to phone booths in post offices
or kiosks rather than the hotel. Dial 00 and then the
country code (UK 44; USA and Canada 1; Australia 61;
New Zealand 64), then dial the number, omitting the
first zero of the area code.

Mobile phones from North America encounter problems in
Europe, so an international mobile phone like the **Mobal World
Phone** (ⓦ www.mobal.com) is highly recommended. This is
advertised as the cheapest way to use mobile phones abroad and
it works in 140 countries once it's set up. There are no minimums,
service charges or fees – you pay only for the calls you make, which
are debited from your credit card. Each user has a lifetime phone
number that can be reached in any of the 140 countries.

Post

Stamps (called *marka* or plural *marke*) can be bought at the *Pošta*
(post office) – look for a sign of a yellow spiral with a triangle on
the end. You can also buy stamps from newsagents and tobacco
kiosks. Postboxes are canary yellow. Stamps for postcards sent
to a destination in the EU cost 3,10kn (take around five days);
postcards to North America cost 3,10kn and take about two weeks.

● Greenery lines the steep old alleyways of Dubrovnik

Letters are priced according to weight and parcels should be left open for inspection by the post office before you send them.

ELECTRICITY

Croatia uses 220 volts and round, two-pin plugs. If you need an adaptor, get one before you leave home.

TRAVELLERS WITH DISABILITIES

It was, ironically, the 1991 war that raised the profile of disabled travellers because of the large number of wounded and physically disabled people that the war created. In larger towns and cities, many public places, such as railway stations and airports, are wheelchair accessible, and there are a growing number of hotels that take wheelchairs into consideration. Tourism offices will generally check accommodation for facilities for a visitor, but it's wise to double-check with the hotel itself.

Additional information in English is published in a guide by **Zajednica Saveza osoba s invaliditetom Hrvatske** (🅰 Savska Cesta 3/1, Zagreb ☏ (385) (0)1 482 9394 🅦 www.soih.hr).

TOURIST INFORMATION

The main tourist information office in Dubrovnik will hand out maps and brochures as well as making bookings for concerts and other events. This office is on the square outside Pile Gate. 🅰 Brsalje 5 ☏ (020) 323 887 🅦 www.tzdubrovnik.hr

To read up further before leaving for Dubrovnik, you can contact the **Croatian National Tourist Office** (🅰 2 Lanchesters, 162–164 Fulham Palace Rd, London W6 9ER ☏ (020) 8563 7979 🅦 http://croatia.hr). Staff will provide answers to questions plus supply brochures, accommodation information and maps.

In Croatia, all towns and regions have tourist information centres but, while they can offer names and addresses for accommodation, many don't book on your behalf.

Most towns and resorts will have a website that you can look up, and most have an English version. Among the best are ⓦ www.adriatica.net, which has general information about Adriatic resorts with an online booking service handling apartments, villas and hotels; ⓦ http://croatia.hr, which is the official website for the Croatian National Tourist Board and offers a large amount of information from history to accommodation and dining to links to other sites; ⓦ www.tzdubrovnik.hr, which is the best of the sites covering Dubrovnik and the surrounding area.

BACKGROUND READING

Balkan Ghosts by Robert Kaplan. As a political look at the tortured politics in the area, Kaplan bases his insightful comments on an extensive trip in 1990. A good read.

Black Lamb and Grey Falcon by Rebecca West. This is one of the classic travel books for the area and it has both fans and detractors. The first quarter of the book is about Croatia.

Café Europa by Slavenka Drakulic. One of Croatia's leading novelists, Drakulic's collection of essays has a section on Croatia and the flowering of nationalism.

Croatia: A Nation Forged in War by Marcus Tanner. An enthusiastic, balanced and thorough look at the general history of Croatia, written by a journalist who witnessed the country's break-up.

Explaining Yugoslavia by John B Allcock. For anyone curious about how such a disparate bunch of nations were pasted together to form Yugoslavia, this is a knowledgeable and stimulating historical account.

Emergencies

The general emergency free-call number is ① 112
Alternatively, you can call: **Police** ① 192 **Emergency** ① 194 **Road help**
① 1987 **Fire brigade** ① 193

MEDICAL SERVICES
Hospital
Roka Mišetića ② Lapad, 4 km (2¹/₂ miles) west of the Old Town
① (020) 431 777 ⓦ www.bolnica-du.hr ① 24-hour service

Pharmacies
There are a dozen or more pharmacies (called *ljekarna*) in Dubrovnik,
with three on Stradun (Placa) alone. These two pharmacies take
turns to be open 24 hours a day:

● *A carved stone on Lopud Island*

EMERGENCY PHRASES

Help!	Please call an ambulance!
Pomoć!	Pozovite hitnu, molim vas!
Po-moch!	*Po-zo-vit-e hi-tnoo, mo-lim vas!*

Kod Zvonika Placa (020) 321 133
Ljekarna Gruž Obala pape Ivana Pavla II 9 (020) 418 990

POLICE
The police are visible everywhere (in their blue uniforms), and occasionally they will stop foreigners to ask for identification: be sure you have your passport or identity card with you at all times. The police are extremely pleasant and helpful to tourists, but not all of them speak English.
Police Station Dr Ante Starčevića 13 (020) 443 777

EMBASSIES & CONSULATES
Although there is a British Consulate in Dubrovnik, most embassies and consulates are in Zagreb:
Australian Embassy Kaptol Centar, 3rd Floor Nova Ves 11, Zagreb (01) 489 12 00 www.croatia.embassy.gov.au
British Consulate Mercante Centar, Vukovarska 22, 1st Floor, Dubrovnik (020) 324 597
British Embassy Ivana Lučića 4, Zagreb (01) 600 91 00 http://ukincroatia.fco.gov.uk
US Embassy 2 Thomas Jefferson Street, Zagreb (01) 661 22 00 http://zagreb.usembassy.gov

ACKNOWLEDGEMENTS
Thomas Cook Publishing wishes to thank the photographers, picture libraries and other organisations, to whom the copyright belongs, for the photographs in this book.

Višnja Arambašić, pages 7 & 109; Darko Barisic, pages 94–5; BigStockPhoto.com (Matthew Ragen, page 24); Croatian National Tourist Board (pages 39, 42–3, 101 & 146; Romeo Ibrisevic, pages 132–3; Juraj Kopac, page 129); Dreamstime.com (Dario Bajurin, page 21; Roman Czupryniak, page 87; Ejla, page 12; Andre Nantel, page 33; Oriontrail, page 61; Nebojsa Tomic, page 71); Dubrovnik-Neretva County Tourist Board, pages 15, 22, 57 & 66; Excelsa nekretnine dd, page 17; Flickr (Guido Merkelbach, page 37); iStockphoto.com (Digital Apoptosis, page 27); Jeroen van Marle, pages 19, 23, 62, 137, 141, 151 & 154; Mestrovic Gallery Archive, page 119; John Smith, pages 69 & 105; SXC.hu (Marinko Bartulovic, page 117; Maciej Perek, page 5; Damian Searles, page 122); Wikimedia Commons (Selby, page 137); Helena Zukowski, all others.

Project editor: Rosalind Munro
Layout: Trevor Double
Proofreaders: Karolin Thomas & Jennifer Jahn

Send your thoughts to
books@thomascook.com

- Found a great bar, club, shop or must-see sight that we don't feature?
- Like to tip us off about any information that needs a little updating?
- Want to tell us what you love about this handy little guidebook and more importantly how we can make it even handier?

Then here's your chance to tell all! Send us ideas, discoveries and recommendations today and then look out for your valuable input in the next edition of this title.

Email the above address (stating the title) or write to:
pocket guides Series Editor, Thomas Cook Publishing, PO Box 227, Coningsby Road, Peterborough PE3 8SB, UK.

WHAT'S IN YOUR GUIDEBOOK?

Independent authors Impartial up-to-date information from our travel experts who meticulously source local knowledge.

Experience Thomas Cook's 165 years in the travel industry and guidebook publishing enriches every word with expertise you can trust.

Travel know-how Thomas Cook has thousands of staff working around the globe, all living and breathing travel.

Editors Travel-publishing professionals, pulling everything together to craft a perfect blend of words, pictures, maps and design.

You, the traveller We deliver a practical, no-nonsense approach to information, geared to how you really use it.

Useful phrases

English	Croatian	Approx pronunciation
BASICS		
Yes	Da	*Da*
No	Ne	*Ne*
Please	Molim	*Mo-lim*
Thank you	Hvala	*Hva-la*
Hello	Zdravo	*Zdra-vo*
Goodbye	Zbogom	*Zbo-gom*
Excuse me	Oprostite	*O-`pro-sti-te*
Sorry	Pardon	*Par-don*
That's OK	To je u redu	*To ye oo re-doo*
I don't speak Croatian	(Ja) ne govorim hrvatski	*(Ya) ne `go-vo-rim `hr-vat-ski*
Do you speak English?	Govorite li engleski?	*`Go-vo-ri-te li `en-gle-ski?*
Good morning	Dobro jutro	*Do-bro yoo-tro*
Good afternoon	Dobar dan	*Do-bar dan*
Good evening	Dobra veĕer	*Do-bra ve-cher*
Good night	Laku noć	*La-koo noch*
My name is ...	Moje ime je ...	*Mo-ye ime ye ...*
NUMBERS		
One	Jedan	*Ye-dan*
Two	Dva	*Dva*
Three	Tri	*Tri*
Four	Četri	*`Che-ti-ri*
Five	Pet	*Pet*
Six	Šest	*Shest*
Seven	Sedam	*Se-dam*
Eight	Osam	*O-sam*
Nine	Devet	*De-vet*
Ten	Deset	*De-set*
Twenty	Dvadeset	*`Dva-de-set*
Fifty	Pedeset	*Pe-`de-set*
One hundred	Sto	*Sto*
SIGNS & NOTICES		
Airport	Aerodrom	*`A-e-ro-drom*
Entrance/Exit	Ulaz/Izlaz	*Oo-laz/Iz-laz*
Smoking/ No smoking	Za pušače/Za nepušače (Zabranjeno pušenje)	*Za poo-`sha-che/Za `ne-poo-sha-che (`Za-bra-nye-no `poo-she-nye)*
Toilets	WC	*Ve tse*
Ladies/Gentlemen	Ženski/Muški	*Zhen-ski/Moosh-ki*